LARS VON TRIER

BREAKING THE WAVES

•

**WRITTEN AND DIRECTED BY**
# LARS VON TRIER

*faber and faber*

# CONTENTS

# PREFACE

*Stig Björkman*

AT THE 1996 CANNES FILM FESTIVAL BREAKING THE WAVES was given a standing ovation by an enthusiastic audience. It was praised by film-makers from all over the world. At the end of the festival, it was awarded the jury's Grand Prize. Yet again Lars von Trier had confirmed his standing as one of today's most important and most innovative artists at the cinema's foremost trade fair, where ten years previously his first feature, THE ELEMENT OF CRIME, had proved a minor sensation, and EUROPA (US title: ZENTROPA) had met with genuine acclaim when it was premiered at Cannes in 1991.

Can we believe in miracles? This is the question Lars von Trier poses with BREAKING THE WAVES. Von Trier himself categorises the film as a sensual melodrama. It is a violent passion play about religious dogmatism and erotic obsession where physical love is endowed with life-giving powers of healing.

The plot makes one recall English 19th century Romantic literature—the Brontë sisters and their occult metaphysics and emotional dramas. Von Trier has indicated two vital sources of inspiration. One is the Danish-American director Douglas Sirk's lofty melodramas of the fifties, the other is Carl Theodor Dreyer's ORDET (THE WORD), also a film about a miracle in a religious community that refuses to accept the inexplicable. The original title of the film was AMOR OMNIE (LOVE IS EVERYTHING), the epitaph the main character in GERTRUD wished to have on her gravestone.

Lars von Trier is indisputably Denmark's most important film director since Dreyer. Paradoxically, there is also much which unites these two apparently so dissimilar artistic temperaments. There is a tautness, an irrepressibility and an obsessiveness which, although expressed in quite different ways, may be seen as a link binding them together. They are a pair of magicians from two different eras, who, with different means but similar earnestness and passion, seek new ways of exploring the nature of the cinema.

A similarity may be sought in what Dreyer saw as the cinema's primary potential for artistic innovation, namely abstraction. In his writings he defines the term 'abstraction' as a measure of the artist's will to abstract himself from reality in order to strengthen his film's cerebral content. The artist must free himself from naturalism in order to expose an inner life. The cinema must move away from being purely imitative art, and the sincere director should seek a higher reality than that attainable by merely picking up his camera and recording reality.

The director may be seen as an explorer of inner and outer landscapes. He has his map, but at the same time remembers that he is his own navigator. No landscape is predetermined. If he wants a jungle, he can allow the vegetation to grow wild. If he is looking for a desert, by the stroke of a pen he can transform a blooming meadow to barren soil.

When I met Lars von Trier in June 1995 a couple of months before he embarked on shooting for BREAKING THE WAVES, the film's atlas had long existed in the form of a bulky script. It describes a small, devoutly religious community in the Outer Hebrides. An introverted society where everyone knows everyone else and no secrets are possible. The islanders regard themselves as God's chosen people and guardians not only of their own morals but perhaps even more of those of their neighbours.

At the centre of the plot is Bess, a young woman raised in this life-denying community. She is the incarnation of goodness. Inno-cent in every way, and greatly affected by her existence in this community pervaded by interdictions and unwavering rules. Rules drawn up and defined by the religious authority, the Council of Elders.

Her encounter with Jan, a man who works on one of the oil rigs, changes her life. Jan is considerably older than Bess. He has seen the world. He has a wealth of experience, not least on the erotic level. His love embodies her liberation. Her love gives Jan an unaccustomed sense of security; his restlessness has hitherto been his greatest sorrow.

Their love is regarded as a provocation and a threat by most of the islanders. Jan is an outsider and an intruder. Bess' transformation through the passion she experiences cannot go unpunished ...

BREAKING THE WAVES is an account of a miracle. The super-natural, of course, has never been alien to Lars von Trier; in this case it involves love as a soothing, healing power. When Jan is paralysed and suffers terrible head injuries in an accident, at his urging Bess gives herself to other men. Her love sacrifice is his re-demption. But it is also her downfall and damnation.

BREAKING THE WAVES preaches a message of atonement with Roman Catholic undertones, but in which sin and punishment are united in an almost ritual invocation of love with as much sensual substance as spiritual character. Lars von Trier, who converted to the Roman Catholic Church a few years ago, has long wanted to make a film on a sharply defined religious issue.

He has elected to make a film about 'goodness'. As a child he had a book called GOLD HEART, about a little girl who went into the woods with some bread and other titbits in her pocket. But at the end of the story, after her journey through the dark woods, she is left naked and with nothing left at all. The book closes with the words 'I'll do all right anyway', said Gold Heart. An expression of the martyr's role taken to its utmost extreme.

'I read the book many times, even though my father regarded it as the worst trash conceivable.' The story of BREAKING THE WAVES probably originates here; Gold Heart is Bess in the film.

She is goodness in its most absolute *gestält*.

One of his first and most overwhelming experiences of the cinema, Lars says, was a 1962 Disney production of a Jules Verne novel, IN SEARCH OF THE CASTAWAYS, a Christmas release in 19th century costumes which took the young heroes halfway round the world in their hunt for their vanished father.

It is not beyond credence that a film like IN SEARCH OF THE CASTAWAYS may have sparked off a film-maker-to-be, even though he was far from the age at which career choices are made. The children in this adventure emerge unscathed from earthquake, flood, typhoon, volcanic eruption, blizzard and dramatic fires. A highly poetic episode takes place in a giant tree where the main characters have sought refuge from a flood which has inundated the entire landscape. They live in peaceful co-existence with wild animals like jaguars, and with crocodiles at the foot of the tree which greedily swallow the message in a bottle that the heroes try to despatch.

'That film contains the inspiration for my entire film output', Lars claims. 'In it you will find the ideas for most of my films'.

Perhaps we should not take him too literally, despite the water-logged settings of THE ELEMENT OF CRIME, EPIDEMIC or MEDEA. Or Rigshospitalet in THE KINGDOM, the unsteady foundations of which rest on the old bleaching meadows. But what IN SEARCH OF THE CASTAWAYS first and foremost has to offer in this Hollywood, over-theme-park-like version is landscapes as an expression of psychological states. It also contains the element of myth and saga which imbues Lars von Trier's work to such a high degree, though the word 'Tale' is perhaps more in keeping with his narrative ambition: for Lars von Trier certainly has tales to tell. Heroic epics and eternal tragedies, fables of horror and sensitive narratives. Tales for the cinema.

BREAKING THE WAVES was shot in summer 1995, in studios in Copenhagen and on location on the Isle of Skye, off the north west coast of Scotland. The Isle of Skye presents a grand, dramatic landscape of extensive heath and massive rock formations, sparse, wild, expressive countryside, a physical expression of the psychological landscapes and emotional tempests in which the leading characters are caught.

Most film units on location in foreign climes seem to the visitor to be happy units. The cast and the team behind the camera are on an extended excursion away from everyday life. They live a kind of unaccustomed holiday existence which also happens to include work and responsibilities. There was also a light euphoria about the unit on the Isle of Skye, despite the forces of nature which contributed biting winds and heavy downpours. The fact that the weather was ideal in terms of the plot was perhaps not always equally convenient to the members of the unit.

I visited them for a couple of the final days of shooting, but euphoria was still the predominant emotion even after three months of intense, exhausting work.

The reason was quite definitely the ease with which Lars von Trier commanded his troops. Unautocratic, and with considerably more extensive delegation of authority than usual. In the wake of THE KINGDOM his relationship to his cast is easier and more trusting. Apparently there used to be a more reserved attitude on Lars' part, a shyness, perhaps even a fear.

If the experimental aspects and complex techniques provided the cohesion in EUROPA, the cast are the source of the tale's constancy in BREAKING THE WAVES. Lars von Trier certainly does not abandon his exploratory ambitions as regards the language of the cinema, though: he decided to shoot BREAKING THE WAVES in CinemaScope with a hand-held camera!

'The hand-held camera gives quite a different feeling of intimacy', Lars says, and refers to Pasolini's films. 'A film must be like a pebble in your shoe.' But he considers that the technique chosen can also give a completely new closeness and documentary feel to the film.

More than anything, the narrative method was chosen in order to put the main focus on the cast. Lars offered them freedom at their own risk and their own responsibility, not least through doing each take under new conditions and the fact that no take was a copy of its predecessor. The cast were encouraged to contribute improvised changes to the acting, expression and intonation when new takes were made of a scene. The cameraman's task was to show the greatest sensitivity vis-à-vis the spontaneous changes in movements and reactions.

One would think that a short visit to a film set would provide the visitor with one or more keys to the finished film. Indeed, in some cases the pattern and context do seem to be transparently clear and obvious. We see them in the directness of the acting, the actors' challenging confrontations with the camera. But most things are hidden in secret, invisible decisions we only discover on the silver screen. It is impossible to imagine a cinematographical work when the flow of time in the picture cannot yet be discerned.

The director has conjured up his setting. He has entered into it with his accomplices and built a house nobody can see into. There a rite is underway, and any outsider is like a tourist equipped with the wrong phrase-book.

The script presented in this book must also be regarded as a kind of semi-manufacture. It merely marks out the foundations of the finished work. It may be viewed as a proposal to be subjected to the interpretations of the other people involved. The finished film is an expression of the highly personal readings of the director, cinematographer, and not least the actors.

A few months later I see the first version of BREAKING THE WAVES, and again it is the actors who take charge from the very first shots. They are the raison d'être of the film. They steer the drama and the fates of their characters with the utmost fidelity and artlessness. In editing the film, Lars von Trier seems to have wanted solely to bring out the most expressive moments, the truest and most intense aspects of their acting. The editing is uniquely audacious. It pays no regard to any given rules at all. It is based directly upon feelings and constantly strives for maximum intensity. This makes the portrayal unusually raw-edged, and at the same time lends it an overwhelming immediacy.

More than anything, this is noticeable in the formation of the portrait of Bess. In Emily Watson's frank impersonation this ingenuous young woman becomes the dynamic hub of the film. Her genius for expressing vulnerability as strength or childishness as a weapon makes her all the more credible. She has a strange, conspiratorial relationship with the camera. Again and again she is caught glancing at the audience as if she wants us to confirm or sanction her actions. And her conversations with God, in which she interprets God's teachings in her own voice, have the same self-evident timbre as the rest of her utterances.

The film picks up and develops themes Lars von Trier often returns to. As in EUROPA and THE KINGDOM a power structure is subjected to a critical gaze; in this case a rigorously religious community with its enforced obedience and ethics based on predestination. Here, too, we arrive at the portals of the inexplicable, the mystic powers which drive the female lead to her acts of charity, the self-sacrificing goodness which contrasts with the seductive, destructive powers of evil. Evil is personified in the film by a recurrent guest in von Trier's works, an actor who often assumes roles with demonic overtones, Udo Kier. It is he who embodies the evil spirit in the story, the new-born monster in the final episode of THE KINGDOM, for example!

BREAKING THE WAVES is a film about miracles, and the frenetic visual storm bestows on it a sense of great dignity. The emotions are more ecstatic and violent than in The Word, Dreyer's drama of redemption. But the agony is similar, also in its overall old-fashionedness. Dreyer invoked his drama in a staging based on long, intense shots which he called 'fluid close-ups'.

Lars von Trier's impatient, nervous hand-held documentation might be called 'fluid close-up reportage'. Obviously taken to extremes, it might be seen as a direct development of Dreyer's challenging defiance of naturalism. For there is the same magic, the same persistently enticing magic, behind what seems to be taking place in those seemingly so transparent images.

*Stig Björkman* (b. 1938) is a Swedish film writer and director. He edited the Swedish film magazine CHAPLIN from 1964 to 1972, and has contributed to other European publications such as the French film magazine CAHIERS DU CINÉMA. He has made shorts, a documentary on Ingmar Bergman, and seven features. He served as the first film consultant in Denmark, and has published books on Ingmar Bergman and Woody Allen.

In 1997 Stig Björkman will be publishing his book VON TRIER ON VON TRIER—CONVERSATIONS WITH STIG BJÖRKMAN.

# THE PICTURES BETWEEN THE CHAPTERS IN BREAKING THE WAVES

*Per Kirkeby*

FOR A LONG TIME THEY WERE CALLED the 'panorama scenes'. Even though the format was the same for every image in the film. All the same, it was easy to understand why; fundamentally it was perfectly obvious that they were intended as the antithesis of the palpitating intrusion of the other images into the tropistic intimacy of the film. They were to be the *view*, the panoramic picture post-card, nature, the archetypal mood, the agonising banality.

As is the case with any work of art, for BREAKING THE WAVES the artist—Lars—knew what he wanted, but not what it looked like. That is why one takes on the job. Otherwise the agonising knowledge cannot be discharged, and one dies. Great insights and questions become quite tangible and manageable.

Steen and Søren sat at the computer to make these few minutes for a great film knowing nothing but that they had to create grand, larger-than-life romantic landscapes. Where was the style? Was it melodramatic, trick photography or what? Machines seem to allow one to do loads of things. Add a few more mountain peaks?

Lars asked me if I'd explain just what romantic paintings had about them. The paintings from history which lurk somewhere in the subconscious, on museum visits, and in any kitsch painting. The painter knows something the machinery with its contrived monocular vision has forgotten: that every painting has more than one focal point. That in a Turner the skies and the mass move about in an 'inner' way, not a mechanical one. All very interesting I am sure, but Steen had to get back to his machine and all the fantastic things it could do but seemingly without making the soul move.

So Lars asked if I'd have a go. Oh, I had a few tricks up my sleeve from living with pictures for so many years, but also a certain contempt—disguised as computer fright—for the tool at hand. But it turned out to be quite simple. My ideas were pretty banal, and as we literally began feeding the machines with the clouds, full moons and rainbows, movement appeared. The classical paradox revealed itself in the picture once again: that a simple conception contains in its visual appearance the richest complexity, and conversely, something produced with great labour and with impressive contributions from many complicated processes merely leaves an easily intelligible feeling of just that: great effort.

But once we were on the track that it was simple and thereby as rich as pencil on paper, Steen was able to open his goody-bag and draw away, with all the possibilities the machine contained. To serve the cause, so to speak.

We created a set which served the purpose of helping Lars figure out what he really wanted. What would be Over The Top, what would be too melodramatic, and so on. There were a couple from our first try that could be used. And so we continued. Until at the very last moment we had them all.

They are not stills, but moving sequences. They all have a pulse beat. Several have dramatic shifts in normally far slower processes, and all this in a time frame of under a minute. Yet most people remember the pictures as motionless. I think this is a sign that they function as they were intended to. They are insidious, so to speak; they leave their symbol-traces unremarked. Their effect lies primarily in the symbolic power of changes in the light. It's an ancient, banal, quite unverbalised message. In a painting, of course, this takes place with infinite subtlety, with the entire process fixed as if by magic on a timeless surface; but precisely by not abhorring any form of banality the mechanical medium was able to take on something of the same quality.

There is stacks of interesting technology involved. Something that made the machinery seem quite human to me, or perhaps animal, rather. We fed the machine with our backdrops. And once we'd marked up the beginnings and the ends of the brief—but lighting-wise big—changes, the machines had the job of forming the whole process. And that took time; they stood there groaning and tramping away for weeks. That was a thought that really appealed to me, and one which in many ways reconciled me to the whole idea of computers.

Then came the far more trivial, error-laden transfer to the film material. But by then I was out of the picture.

*Per Kirkeby* (b. 1938) primarily a painter, but also a sculptor, writer and film-maker.

# A STORY ABOUT
# PEOPLE AND EMOTIONS

BREAKING THE WAVES is Lars von Trier's fifth feature film and is entirely different from his previous work. Shot in English on locations in Denmark and Scotland—the Isle of Skye and both of Scotland's north east and west coasts—the film, von Trier's most accessible to date, is a love story aimed at a wide international audience.

The story is set in the early 1970s amid a small tightly knit community on the remote north coast of Scotland and tells of Bess, a young naive innocent girl and her profound experience of love. Bess, who has lived her life protected by her family within the confined world of strict Calvinism, falls is love with Jan, a stalwart oil-rig worker and man-of-the-world. Despite local opposition, the couple marry. Shortly after the wedding Jan has to return to the rig, leaving Bess to count the days to their reunion. Bess is sure that their love is made in Heaven, especially as she is convinced she can mentally communicate with God. When an accident renders Jan bedridden he pleads that Bess should prove the true love and devotion that she feels for him by continuing regardless with her own life.

Von Trier describes the film as 'a simple love story, something I would never have considered a few years ago, but now I wanted to make a film for audiences who want to see human emotions from identifiable people made of flesh and blood.'

BREAKING THE WAVES is produced by Zentropa Entertainments (Denmark) which has been run by Lars von Trier and producer Peter Aalbaek Jensen since 1992, and Trust Film (Sweden) run by Lars Jonsson. Previous productions have included such films as Lars von Trier's THE KINGDOM and Colin Nutley's HOUSE OF ANGELS.

Producer Vibeke Windeløv explains that an initial difficulty in raising the budget stemmed from von Trier's change of direction. Following the international recognition of, and many prizes won by, ELEMENT OF CRIME and EUROPA, would-be financiers seemed reluctant to accept von Trier's determination to film a love story. She explained that they had been working on raising the money for the film for some time, but it was not until the outstanding success of his television series, THE KINGDOM, that the funding fell into place. Made for Danish television, it broke all ratings records in Denmark, where the streets of Copenhagen became deserted on transmission nights.

The assistance of Scottish Film Services was instrumental in the production choosing Scotland as a location. Lars von Trier, who is based in Copenhagen and hates to travel, felt immediately at home in the Scottish landscape with the sudden weather changes. The bleakness of the landscape and constantly changing light was precisely what the storyline called for.

Set in a remote village where life is hard and the inhabitants practise an extremely rigid form of the Protestant religion, frowning on alcohol, music, dancing and ever declaring Church bells to be 'man's work, not God's' with no qualms about exiling any members who break their rules. Although the original story was set in a fishing community on the West Coast of Denmark, where the strict Puritan church of the 'Inner Mission' holds sway, it is mirrored in a similar bleak religion in Scotland, the 'Free Church' which has a tight grip on the population of the Western Isles.

'In remote communities, where daily life is tough,' explains von Trier, 'a rigid support is necessary, keeping the community together by persuading them that God is forever scrutinising their behaviour, and any misdemeanour has to be punished by ex-communication to protect the others. Because, in the script, Bess interprets the results of her acts as a miracle, the religion portrayed had to be one where miracles are not only not recognised but rejected as Satan's work.'

Once the finance was in place, and the decision made to locate the film in Scotland, casting could be undertaken.

Although the language of the film is English, there is a distinct but comprehensible Scottish accent. Elspeth MacNaughton, a dialect specialist, was brought on board to coach the actors and was also present during the shooting.

In choosing his cast, the lack of American finance meant that the director was free of the usual 'box-office' constraints that are normally behind the final choice of the lead actors. Whilst Bess and the other villagers were to be cast from British actors, von Trier was able to cast the oil rig, being an international community, from an interesting range of actors: Scandinavians, Stellan Skarsgård and Mikkel Gaup, alongside American-Frenchman Jean-Marc Barr and Dutchman Reof Ragas, were cast as the oil-rig workers.

For the lead role of Bess, von Trier is thrilled to have discovered British actress Emily Watson. 'We had auditions with many young actresses, but as soon as I saw Emily on tape I knew that we had found Bess. Emily has a face that expresses an enormous range of emotion; a face that you can never tire of watching.'

Playing opposite Bess, as Jan her husband, a man who is older and more worldly wise, von Trier chose Swedish actor Stellan Skarsgård. 'As a worker on the oil rig, he is an outsider to this close community. He is also weary of his gypsy existence and ready to settle down with someone he sees as an angel.'

In addition to his busy schedule of film, stage and television roles in Scandinavia, Skarsgård is known to international audiences for his performances in THE HUNT FOR RED OCTOBER and THE UNBEARABLE LIGHTNESS OF BEING.

Following his success in EUROPA, French American actor, Jean-Marc Barr was pleased to be reunited with von Trier. Barr

17

achieved international box office success in Luc Besson's THE BIG BLUE in 1988 and accepted the lead in EUROPA in 1990, recognising von Trier as a director with a special voice and EUROPA as a film which demanded more of an audience than any of the American films he was being offered. He had no hesitation in accepting a role in BREAKING THE WAVES.

The casting of Katrin Cartlidge in the role of Dodo, Bess' overprotective sister-in-law, is a change of pace for the actress, who is more often cast as a wild and irresponsible character. Since her performance in Mike Leigh's award winning NAKED, Cartlidge has chosen to work with some of Europe's most innovative directors, appearing in BEFORE THE RAIN (winner of the Golden Lion at Venice) for director Milcho Manchevski and THREE STEPS TO HEAVEN directed by Constantine Gianaris. The cast is rounded out by a collection of the best of British and European character actors.

English and Scottish walk-ons resident in Denmark also took part. At the Danish Film Studios at Lyngby, a church interior was constructed on the biggest sound stage. The wedding reception and all of the hospital interiors were also shot in Denmark.

Once again, Lars von Trier employs innovative technology. Shooting always on hand-held cameras gives his actors freedom to move around in a scene, with no restrictions, as if they were on a limitless stage. And shooting outdoors in Northern Scotland in October meant exposure to a wide range of weather conditions— all day, every day.

The director recognised that matching weather in shots would not only be time-consuming but unrealistic. Shot in super-35mm based cinemascope, which will then be transferred to digital format, the action will be interspersed with panorama shots of the locations, which will be painted to become high resolution 'picture postcard perfect' in contrast to the rest of the film. These interludes are described by von Trier as 'God's-eye-view of the landscape in which this story is unfolding, as if he were watching over the characters'.

The director had discussed the project a few years earlier with Dutch cinematographer Robby Müller, whose work with Wim Wenders and Jim Jarmusch von Trier admired. Müller was happy to accept the position of Director of Photography and embrace the challenges of shooting with only a hand-held camera. 'We have to light 360 degrees, as the camera will follow the actor in any direction during a scene. It is a challenging production which, for me, makes it very exciting.'

The close-to-present-day setting of the film, which von Trier believes that an audience will accept more readily given the authenticity of another specific time and place, presented the production with more than a few headaches. Because it is within living memory costume detail is very important and Scotland was scoured for period cars and transport—twenty year-old mass-market vehicles that have not been up-dated were advertised for and auditioned.

The soundtrack uses to great effect the popular music of the early 1970s from David Bowie, Elton John, Deep Purple, T-Rex, Procul Harum and Roxy Music with a theme tune written by Joachim Holbeck, who previously collaborated with von Trier on the score of THE KINGDOM.

# DIRECTOR'S NOTE - THIS FILM IS ABOUT 'GOOD'

*Lars von Trier*

FOR A LONG TIME I have been wanting to conceive a film in which all driving forces are 'good'. In the film there should only be 'good', but since the 'good' is misunderstood or confused with something else, because it is such a rare thing for us to meet, tensions arise.

The character of Bess is 'good' in a spiritual sense ... living mostly in the world of her imagination, never really accepting that things apart from 'good'; might exist. She is a strong person taking full responsibility of her own life, even though others might think that she is not capable of doing so. Bess is made strong by her belief and by her love. So strong that she masters even rebellion against the strict suppressing rules of the little community and the church that once was so dear to her.

Jan is 'good' in a much more difficult way—because he consciously aims to do 'good'. He inhabits the real world, where doing 'good' is of course much harder.

The fact that he falls in love and marries simple-minded Bess, whom no other man wants, is an example of his fidelity to his feelings, the will to do 'good' or 'right'; if he loves somebody, society or the opinions of other people should never be allowed to interfere.

Jan has strict ideas about love and how love should be lived. He is a man of experience and has always lived by his 'love-sick bed he experiences bitterness ... the most natural feeling in the world in his situation ... but to Jan it is a new feeling and not easily reconcilable with his philosophy of life—and a feeling that terrifies him.

He is doped up and once after a drugged night's sleep he wakes from a bad dream. In the dream he was not himself. We have all had this experience ... a dream where your actions and desires are unfamiliar and frightening. For Jan, who wants to do 'good' this is terrible.

When he is most affected by his brain damage and medication, he is unable to control himself, and in his stupor will say things that Bess, simple-minded as she is, will believe are coming from the other Jan ... the sane Jan that she loves, not the confused mixture of subconscious fragments, fear and 'drunkenness' from the mind of an hallucinating, dying man.

In his moments of clarity he is deeply perturbed and weeps at the effect he may have had on Bess while unconscious. Soon he knows that a forced separation between him and Bess is her only salvation.

By trying to save her, he loses her. By doing 'good'! By trying to save him, by doing 'good', the world that she loved turned against her.

But the 'good' will always be recognised ... somewhere!

*Copenhagen, March 1995*

# BREAKING THE WAVES
## MANUSCRIPT

*(Often Bess will, as the only person, look directly into the camera during the film. She will look without leaving her mood or motivation.)*

**Scene 1.** EXT. PATH BY THE CLIFFS. DAY
*A small woman walks along a path on a sea cliff. It is Bess. She is tiny but there is something strong and intense about her. She looks at the water. She is lost in her own thoughts and the image of the water. Suddenly she wakes up.*

BESS  Are you still there?
    (in a gruff voice) What is it now Bess?
    (in her own voice) There is something else ...
    (in a gruff voice) Yes?
    (in her own voice) I would like to marry Jan ...
    (in a gruff voice) You have already asked the elders, haven't you?
    (in her own voice) Well, yes ... I just wanted to tell you ...

**Scene 2.** INT. CHURCH. CHURCH HALL. NIGHT
*The twelve elders are sitting around the big table. They are all men. One of them is the Minister. One of the twelve is rocking on his chair.*

*Otherwise there is silence. William, an elderly, greying, rather tor-
mented-looking man, looks around a little. He looks at the rocker,
but the chairman of the council of elders does not return his glance.
William clears his throat.*

WILLIAM I must submit to the council that my grand-daughter
   has expressed her desire to be wed.


*The gathering is astonished by this intelligence. A couple of its mem-
bers smile as if William's words were a joke. The chairman looks at
William.*

CHAIRMAN William McNiell, your grand-daughter is a half-wit.
   No local man has ever expressed any desire to marry poor
   Bess, and I cannot conceive of any man in his right mind ever
   doing so.

WILLIAM (quietly) He is not a local man.

*The elders look at one another.*

CHAIRMAN (sharply) I appreciate your desire to see your grand-
   daughter wed, William. We are all very fond of her, but marriage to an outsider would only bring her sorrow and bitterness. I suppose he is from the rig?

WILLIAM Bess's faith is strong, and no man can deny it. I am also
   against matches to outsiders, but fate has nevertheless decreed
   that for a second time I must ask this council to look kindly
   on just such a match. To date God has not granted Bess much
   happiness or brain power ...

CHAIRMAN Has the man agreed to enter into holy matrimony.
   under the articles and conventions of our church?

WILLIAM Yes.

CHAIRMAN Which church does he belong to?

WILLIAM None, so far as I am aware.

CHAIRMAN None?

AN ELDER (with a smile) You'd prefer a Catholic, perhaps?

CHAIRMAN Has it occurred to you, William, that if the Lord
   were to bless such a marriage with offspring ...

WILLIAM Bess cannot have children.

CHAIRMAN (nods slightly) Is she present?

WILLIAM (straightens) Bess is here!

CHAIRMAN Fetch her in.

*William gets up slowly and goes out. He returns with Bess. She is small, but she radiates strength. She stands calmly before the council. She smiles.*

CHAIRMAN Bess McNiell, I understand you wish to wed?

*She nods. She smiles.*

CHAIRMAN Wed whom?

BESS His name is Jan.

CHAIRMAN I do not know him.

BESS He is from the rig.

CHAIRMAN (nods) You know that we do not enter into matrimony with outsiders.

BESS Dodo's from outside!

CHAIRMAN Yes, we consented to that match, as she had embraced our church, and we saw that she could become one of us.

AN ELDER Bess McNiell, can you even tell us what matrimony is?

*The councillors wait tensely for Bess's answer.*

BESS (after a long pause for thought) When two people are joined in God.

AN ELDER Do you realise that you will have to take responsibility for this man too, should the council of elders consent to this marriage? Bess McNiell, do you really believe you are capable of bearing the responsibility not only for your own marriage in God, but also another's?

BESS (with absolute certainty) I know I am!

CHAIRMAN Your petition is a grave matter, Bess McNiell. We seldom consent to these mixed marriages. I have to say that none has ever proved a happy one. Can you think of anything of real value the outsiders have brought with them?

BESS (smiles) Their music?

*The chairman looks at her angrily. She beams up at him. He cannot break her smile. He shrugs his shoulders.*

CHAIRMAN Out you go, Bess, and be seated.

*Bess leaves slowly, beaming all the way.*

**Scene 3**. INT. CHURCH. VESTIBULE. NIGHT

*Bess emerges from the church hall. Smiling, she closes the door behind her and sits down on a bench in the deserted vestibule. She goes on smiling for ages.*

*(Suggested music: 'A Whiter Shade of Pale', Procol Harum. Underlies the following scenes, ending on panorama scene 12—helicopter platform)*

**Scene 4**. PANORAMA SCENE

*The church, the minister's house, and the telephone kiosk, deep beneath us in the mountains. Morning.*

OPENING CREDITS
WHITE LETTERING ON BLACK BACKGROUND.

**Scene 5**. PANORAMA SCENE

*The oil rig, a tiny dot in the endless sea. Morning.*

**Scene 6.** INT. RIG. JAN'S CABIN. MORNING

*Jan is putting on morning dress. Terry and Pits are already in theirs. Jan's cabin is small. They are smoking a joint. They offer Jan a drag. He does not take it. They go out together.*

**Scene 7**. INT. RIG. CHANGING ROOMS. MORNING

*Jan, Terry and Pits pull survival suits over their morning dress.*

**Scene 8**. EXT. RIG. MORNING

*The three men wander towards the helicopter platform. The other members of the rig crew knowwhat's going on. They wave and smile.*

**Scene 9.** EXT. RIG. HELICOPTER DECK. MORNING

*The three men wait for the helicopter.*

**Scene 10.** INT. HELICOPTER. MORNING

*The three men laugh and josh on the helicopter. Jan is the oldest and the calmest.*

**Scene 11**. PANORAMA SCENE
*The helicopter on its way across the sea. Day.*


**Scene 12**. EXT. HELIPORT. DAY
*Bess is shivering as she waits in her wedding dress at the heliport beside the shipyards where they repair the rigs brought in from the ocean. Dodo is holding a raincoat round her shoulders. Bess shakes her head.*
**DODO** He will come. Take it easy now.
*Dodo looks at her seriously. Bess is angry. Dodo looks at her watch, then she puts her arms around Bess and holds her tight. A couple of cars of other members of the wedding party are waiting. Someone puts up an umbrella to protect Bess's lovely dress. Everyone is shivering. At last they hear the helicopter, far away. Infinitely slowly it approaches and lands. Jan is the first off in his clumsy survival suit. He waves. Bess looks at him from her shelter a little way off. She loves him. Suddenly she tears herself away from Dodo. She rushes across to Jan while the rotor-blades are still spinning. She is furious. She beats at him with her fists.*
**BESS** Late, late, late!
*He fends her off. Terry and Pits climb down from the helicopter, laughing. They remove their survival suits in the shelter of umbrellas, revealing their morning dress. Jan is given a break to get his own suit off. Everyone gets into the cars and sets off.*


**Scene 13**. PANORAMA SCENE
*Helicopter platform and some of the shipyards. The chopper takes off and the cars roll away. Day.*


**Scene 14**. INT. CHURCH. DAY
*They are inside the church now. Jan can't restrain a laugh when he sees Terry. Bess hits him again. Jan is in his place and Bess is ready to be given away by Grand-dad William. He puts a protective arm around her and gives her a little hug as the organ strikes up*


**Scene 15**. INT. CHURCH. DAY
*Bess and Jan get married. In the middle of the service Bess begins to*

cry far too soon, making the ceremony hard to complete. Jan scowls at Terry. Bess leans on Jan. He is puzzled by all these tears. Dodo sniffles, too. All the girls look at Bess as she passes. She embraces them all at once. She also embraces her mother.

BESS Oh, Mother ...

### Scene 16. EXT. CHURCH. DAY

*Outside the church is the little forecourt with the minister's house and the red telephone kiosk When BESS comes out to throw her bouquet, all the girls flock round her. She gives it a big throw, too high because the wind just catches it, and sends it sailing onto the top of the red telephone kiosk, where it looks odd and out-of-place. Jan embraces Bess. Terry and Pits has followed them out of the church. They are in a good mood now out of the embrace of the church room. A verger is waiting outside the church.*

TERRY (merrily, to the verger) Ring the bells then!

VERGER (courteously) Our church has no bells.

*Jan looks up and sees that the bell tower on the church roof is indeed empty. Bess smiles and pulls Jan away with her.*

### Scene 17. INT. HOTEL. ASSEMBLY ROOMS. DAY

*The wedding reception is taking place in the hotel assembly rooms. Bess is circulating, her arm draped round Dodo. A small electric band is accompanying—badly—a man in a kilt who is playing the bagpipes. Bess and Dodo bump into Sybilla, another girl from the town, dolled up unlike almost everyone else in a super short mini dress and tight blouse. They tease her a little, she grins back. They greet Dr. Richardson, who has his arm round another girl. They look at Jan, who is engaged in conversation with an elderly lady.*

BESS (giggles) He's had a hundred women.

DODO (frowns) Sure!

*Dodo looks Jan up and down. She looks severely at Bess.*

BESS I am so happy!

*Bess embraces Dodo again. They go over to Jan.*

BESS This is my sister in law. She works at the hospital.

*Jan extends his hand to Dodo.*

JAN I don't believe we've met.

DODO (a little shyly) No, everything happened so quickly!

BESS What makes you say that?

*Bess frowns.*

DODO You know very well what I mean. Not a word do you tell me, and then all of a sudden you're getting married to this fellah.

*Dodo walks away from them, tears in her eyes. Bess is vexed.*

BESS Oh, so I'm not old enough, maybe?

*She watches her and is lost for a second in her own thoughts. Then she seeks out Jan's eyes.*

### Scene 18. INT. HOTEL. ASSEMBLY ROOMS. DAY
*The party is in full swing. Jan arm-wrestles with several guests. He wins every time. Bess laughs. A crowd of children has gathered round them. They laugh. The only beverage to be seen is fruit juice. William and four other elders are sitting in the background behind a table. They watch Jan and Bess's table. William and Bess exchange glances. Terry pulls a few bottles of beer out of a bag. He opens one and pours out a glass. He offers it to Jan, but Jan looks around and shakes his head. Bess smiles at Jan and leads him away from the table proudly. She embraces a couple of bride's maids on the way.*

### Scene 19. INT. HOTEL. ASSEMBLY ROOMS. DAY
*Bess dances with Jan. He looks at her smiling while she is moving to the music. She is in a childish kind of trance. Most people smile at her way of giving in to the rhythm. Dr. Richardson is among the guests. He also looks at her, smiling.*

### Scene 20. INT. HOTEL. TOILETS. DAY
*Bess pulls Jan into the Ladies. Then into one of the cubicles. Jan looks at her, laughing. They kiss.*

BESS Have me now.

JAN (astonished) Here?

*Bess nods and smiles.*

BESS Have you never done it like this?

JAN If it was so important to wait until we were married ... maybe

you'd like it a bit more ... romantic.

BESS (pulls him to her, giggling) ... this is a palace ... and the sheets are made of silk ...

*She has closed her eyes. He looks at her while he makes love to her carefully. She smiles all the time. Now he closes his eyes. She looks at him as he comes. He opens his eyes and notices that she is looking at him with a smile.*

JAN (smiling) You are a silly little thing ...

BESS (severely) Not silly!

JAN Not silly ... funny ...

BESS (brightens into a smile) That's right, funny!

*She kisses him. She goes out to the wash basins. He stands there, rather nonplussed, and watches her. She peeps out of the door to see if anyone is coming. She waves Jan out with a grin. He runs past the wash basins as he does up his trousers. Bess pushes him out of the door. She turns on the tap and begins to wash blood off her dress. Dodo is on her way in. She notices Bess and the spot of blood. She closes the door again quietly.*

**Scene 21**. INT. HOTEL. ENTRANCE HALL. DAY

*Dodo is waiting for Bess outside the door. When Bess comes out, Dodo puts her arms round her. They cry together.*

**Scene 22**. INT. HOTEL. ASSEMBLY ROOMS. DAY

*Dodo is standing near the stage with a piece of paper. She is nervous.*

ONE FROM THE BAND (into the mike) Ladies and gentlemen, some loving words from Bess' sister-in-law.

*Dodo speaks from the floor in front of the stage.*

DODO Where I come from there is always a speech for the bride. Since nobody else seems to have anything to say, I will. (looks at her cribsheet) Dear Bess. You have a good heart. You proved that to me when I came here and married your brother. It was not easy coming from the outside as you know, but your warm welcome made me believe that there was a way. You have a good heart and sometimes it is a little too good. Like when you gave your ticket away to somebody who, I'm sure, needed it badly, and had to walk all the way home. I yelled at you then and many times more and now I'm sorry for that, because every time I myself almost gave up living in this cold place, that very generosity of yours helped me through. Thank you for that Bess. When Sam died and I had no husband and you had no brother we promised to look after one another. You have always made me feel like a part of this place and this family. Your good heart is to blame for me staying here and now for somebody else joining the family. His name is Jan. I do not know him. But I must accept his right to be here because I believe in you Bess. He must be all right. And if he is not, and if he does not take care of you and give you all the things that you need, and keep you warm at nights ... (smiling)

I think I will kill him.—Thank you Bess for all that you have given me. I love you very much.

*There has been a little laughter here and there in the crowd, but mostly the words have been received with little joy, especially at the table with the elders. Bess is crying now and is hugging Dodo. Jan looks at the two.*

**Scene 23**. INT. HOTEL. ASSEMBLY ROOMS. DAY

*Terry gets up from his table. He goes to the table where the elders are sitting. He sits down in front of them. He opens a can of beer and empties it in one go with beer running over his face. One of the elders raises and empties a glass of fruit juice the same way. Terry looks at him smiling. Then he squeezes the can flat in his hand. The old man looks calmly at Terry. He raises his empty glass and squeezes it till it breaks. His hand is bleeding but he does not for a second take his calm eyes away from Terry. Terry sits for a second, then he starts to laugh. Nobody else at the table laughs.*

**Scene 24**. EXT. HOTEL. EVENING

*Outside the hotel, which is on the outskirts of town, Jan's big car is waiting. It has been decorated. Tin cans have been tied to the bumper. Jan and Bess are led out to the car by guests from the reception. Jan looks at the car.*

JAN Just a minute.

*He unties the cans from the bumper. He ties them to his belt. Then he picks Bess up. To him she is as light as a feather. He begins to carry her. Some guests accompany them, cheering him on. Bess laughs. Jan breaks into a run. Gradually their train drops away. Bess is spellbound by his strength.*

### Scene 25. PANORAMA SCENE

*LS of the strand promenade. We can just discern Jan as he carries Bess at a run past the houses in the dying rays of the sun. Evening.*

### Scene 26. PANORAMA SCENE

*High above the town, the first street and house lights appearing. We can still hear the faint clank of cans on tarmac. Evening.*

### Scene 27. INT. FLAT. BATHROOM. NIGHT

*Jan sits naked on the edge of the bed. He is smoking and drinking a can of beer. Bess is undressing. She is smiling and looking at him. She is doing it slow. He smiles at her. As she is all naked she comes close to him on the floor. She stops and looks at him.*

BESS Here I am.

JAN Yes.

*They both smile.*

BESS You must teach me everything.

JAN You teach me!

*He kisses her and caresses her. He grows grave.*

JAN You are good. At everything. You are fantastic. You know. Whatever anyone else says, you are good.

*She smiles. He pulls her down towards him. He wants to get on top of her.*

JAN I'm afraid I'll break you.

BESS Please do!

*They kiss. Suddenly she stops short. They sit there for ages, gazing at one another. A profound, silent contact.*

JAN How did you stand it? How were you able to keep away from the boys?

BES I waited for you. And then I found you.

36

JAN (shaking his head) You must have been lonely. Who have you talked to all these years?

*He caresses her.*


**Scene 28.** INT. CHURCH. DAY

*Bess is kneeling in church, her eyes closed. She is whispering.*

BESS (in her own voice) I thank you for the greatest gift of all, the gift of love. I thank you for Jan. I am so lucky to be given these gifts … (in an assumed gruff voice) But remember to be a good girl, Bess, for you know I giveth and I taketh away … (in her own voice, frightened) I didn't mean it like that! Yes, I'll be good! I'll be really good, really, really good …


**Scene 29.** INT. FLAT. DAY

*Bess and Jan are making love again. Bess opens her eyes and looks to the ceiling. She smiles.*

BESS (whispers) Thank you.

*Jan opens his eyes and looks at her. He stops.*

JAN What did you say?

BESS (smiles) Thank you.

JAN Thank you?

*Jan laughs and shakes his head. He hugs her tight and kisses her.*


**Scene 30.** EXT. CHURCH. DAY

*Jan has brought Bess to church. He looks up at the empty bell tower.*

JAN Why don't you have any bells?

BESS Oh, they took them down. Long, long ago.

JAN Why?

*At that moment the minister emerges from his little house.*

MINISTER Bells are man's work. We do not need bells in our church to worship God.

BESS (whispers) I heard church bells once. I never heard anything so beautiful.

*Bess smiles and kisses Jan.*

BESS (giggles) What do you think? We can put them back again?

*Jan gets into the car.*

**Scene 31**. INT. CHURCH. DAY
*Bess goes to communion.*

**Scene 32**. INT. CHURCH. DAY
*Later, during the service. The minister preaches in Gaelic. Sybilla and another girl are standing at the back of the church. They are whispering.*
**SYBILLA** (in a whisper) Do you think he made her happy?
*Another member of the congregation turns angrily on them and they fall silent. Then the congregation begins to sing. Bess sings along.*
**BESS** And though they take our life, goods, honour, children, wife.
  Yet is their profit small, these thing shall vanish all.
*She is as radiant as a little sun, and her voice rings out above the others. Sybilla looks at her and gives her girlfriend a knowing glance. Her girlfriend nods. They giggle. Bess sees them. For a moment it makes her hesitate. And then she goes on singing.*

**Scene 33.** INT. FLAT. NIGHT
*Jan and Bess are sitting eating fish and chips. He looks at her while eating.*
**JAN** Prick.
*He pronounces the word slowly and clearly. She shakes her head.*
**JAN** (patiently) Prick!
*She tries to form the word on her lips but it's still no good.*
**JAN** (smiles) Come on!
**BESS** (almost inaudibly) Prick.
*Instantly she covers her face with her hands, pleasurably bashful.*
**JAN** Never use another word.

**Scene 34.** PANORAMA SCENE
*LS of the lighthouse on its distant peak. Evening.*
**Scene 35**. PANORAMA SCENE
*LS of the fellside. All the nests and the birds in the foreground. Evening.*

**Scene 36**. INT. SMALL CINEMA. NIGHT

*Bess and Jan are sitting in the small local cinema. They are watching a cartoon. It is Bambi. Bess is watching open-mouthed. She is really drawn into the film. To her the experience is enormous. She enjoys every second of it. Jan is looking at her. He is fascinated by her childish joy at the film. He sits for a long time just looking at her. She smiles when the animals are doing cute things and looks serious when something more dramatic is happening. Now she feels his eyes upon her. She turns around to him. She sees that he is watching her. She smiles. A beautiful smile so full of love, never for one second ashamed of the feelings that she expressed toward the cartoon characters. He smiles at her. Just a little, like wanting to excuse for himself, for having looked at her. A little ashamed of looking into her world, a world that he feels he has no right to share. Bess takes his hand and turns towards the screen again. Still with the smile that tells him that she loves him, and loves to share with him. Jan looks at her a little while longer. Then he also looks at the screen. He finds it difficult to relate to the cuteness of the coloured world.*

**Scene 37**. EXT. CEMETERY. DAY

*It's windy in the cemetery, which lies right down beside the sea, independently of the church. Dodo, Jan and Bess are standing beside a group of headstones. Bess has brought flowers. Dodo takes them from her and arranges them beneath a net to stop them from blowing away. Bess smiles.*

BESS (laughs) Here lies father and here lies Sam. They are looking out to sea.

JAN (to Dodo) He worked on the rigs ... your husband?

DODO He got crushed by the drill.

*Bess runs to Jan and embraces him. She teases him a little. She laughs and kisses him.*

**Scene 38**. EXT. OUTSIDE CEMETERY. DAY

*Dodo, Bess and Jan are sitting on a bench on a slope above the cemetery. They are gazing out to sea. Jan's car is parked nearby.*

DODO (looking in the direction of a small funeral gathering a little further away) They're burying Anthony now.

*Jan and Bess look, too. The coffin is about to being lowered into the ground.*

BESS (whispering to Jan with a smile) Go and listen to the minister.

*Jan looks at her and Dodo quizzically. Dodo nods.*

DODO You can do that. Men are allowed to join the train.

*Reluctantly, Jan walks over to the cemetery.*

## Scene 39. EXT. CEMETERY. DAY

*Jan takes up position a little way from the gathering. One man scowls at him. The minister concludes the order of the burial of the dead.*

MINISTER Anthony Dod Mantle you are a sinner and you deserve your place in hell.

*The family bow their heads.*

## Scene 40. EXT. OUTSIDE CEMETERY. DAY

*Jan returns to Dodo and Bess in discomfort.*

JAN He said he would go to hell. Sounds really bloody cheerful.

DODO (shocked) Did he say that?

JAN (nods) I reckon his relatives should have found another vicar.

BESS (shrugs her shoulders) Anthony will go to hell, everyone knows that.

Jan looks at Bess, bewildered.

## Scene 41. EXT. OUTSIDE CEMETERY. DAY

*Jan, Bess and Dodo walks towards the car. Jan puts his arm round Bess.*

JAN (gravely) You do realise I will have to go back, don't you?

*Bess looks furious in a very child-like way. She gets up, runs away, and squats with her back to Dodo and Jan.*

JAN (to Dodo) It's the day after tomorrow.

*Jan goes over to Bess. She is curled right up. He holds her.*

JAN You knew all the time.

## Scene 42. PANORAMA SCENE

*LS of cemetery by the water, with Jan's car parked on the roadside. In*

*the foreground a small bush, whose leaves are being torn off by the
wind. Day.*

**Scene 43**. INT. BESS'S MOTHER'S HOUSE. NIGHT
*Bess and Jan have come for supper. Dodo and Grand-father William
are there, too. They say grace.*
WILLIAM Bless the food that we eat and ourselves to thy service ...
*They eat.*
WILLIAM (to Jan) When are you going back?
*Before Jan can answer, Bess interrupts.*
BESS Didn't you know? Jan is going to quit the rig and stay at
home with me because we're so happy.
*She smiles.*
JAN (beseechingly) Bess!
(To the others) If only I could!
*They eat in silence. Bess begins to cry. She gets up and runs out. Her
mother gets up and follows her.*

**Scene 44.** INT. BESS'S MOTHER'S HOUSE. UPSTAIRS. NIGHT
*In a first floor bedroom Bess is sitting on the bed, staring out of the
window. Her mother comes in.*
BESS´S MOTHER (very angry) I will not have that kind of behavi-
our in my house.
BESS I'm sorry, but I am so sad.
BESS´S MOTHER I've told you I don't want any more of your
moods. If you can't control your moods it's the hospital for
you again, my girl!
BESS I'm sorry, mother.
BESS´S MOTHER Why should you be any different? Every other
woman here has to endure being alone when her husband is at
sea or out on the rigs ...
BESS I'm sorry, I'm sorry ...
BESS´S MOTHER Learning what love is takes time. Being alone
may just help you learn. You must learn too. To endure.

**Scene 45.** INT. BESS'S MOTHER'S HOUSE. NIGHT

*William picks up the newspaper and goes into the living room. Dodo remains at the table with Jan. He looks apologetic. She gives him a determined look.*

DODO If you harm her I won't be responsible for my actions!

JAN (looks up) It's my job ...

DODO That's not what I mean. You are a good-looking bloke. I'm sure you could have got whole bevies of young girls to marry you. So why choose Bess?

JAN I love her.

DODO It's a mystery to me why a bloke like you would marry such a halfwit of a girl.

JAN Is that what she is to you? A 'halfwit'?

DODO Bess isn't well. As you very well know. She's not right in the head. I've had to look out for her, she's very, very susceptible. You can get her to do anything.

JAN (smiling) You think so?

DODO I have been looking out for her ever since I married into this family. She just couldn't take all that ... severity.

JAN I understand that you love her very much ... so do I. I would never do her any harm. I have known other women ... Bess is something special. She is so special.

DODO Just who are you?

JAN I'm an old bastard who's beginning to find it hard to keep up with the youngsters. I've also seen enough to know that Bess is a fantastic woman. And now she is my wife.

DODO How am I to look out for her now?

JAN Listen, Bess is so full of love—and she just couldn't let it out by sticking around here with you.

DODO Love. That's when the trouble starts ... she just hasn't the strength.

JAN She is stronger than you or me.

DODO She's sick in the head!

JAN (laughs) She just wants it all!

**Scene 46**. INT. FLAT. DAY

*Jan is standing outside their flat, his bag packed. Bess and Dodo are there, too. Jan gives Bess a parcel. She opens it greedily. It's a T-shirt and a short dress. She runs upstairs. Dodo looks at Jan, who smiles. Bess comes back in her new clothes. Jan gives her a smile. She embraces him happily.*

*(Suggested music: 'Angie', the Stones. Underlies the following scenes, concluding at start of Panorama scene  LS heliport)*

**Scene 47**. EXT. FLAT. DAY

*Terry and Pits arrive in Jan's big estate. Jan and Bess hop in.*

**Scene 48**. INT. CAR. DAY

*Bess snuggles up close to Jan during the drive. They kiss. She holds his hand so tightly that it hurts him to drive. They drive along the coast. They pass a shipyard where one of the enormous rigs is being completed. Bess catches sight of it. Jan puts an arm around her. Now she begins to cry. He stops the car.*

**Scene 49**. EXT. SHIPYARD. DAY

*Jan and Bess go for a little walk down by the shipyard. He has his arm round her  shoulders. She stops crying. Suddenly she tears herself away from him. She runs down to one of the huge legs and begins hitting it desperately with a spanner. Some shipyard workers have appeared. They watch her performance curiously. Jan kisses her hard. He takes her up a flight of stairs.*

**Scene 50**. INT. CHAMBER. DAY

*In a small room in the rig they come together. They make love violently and sweatily.*

**Scene 51**. EXT. CAR. DAY

*When they get back to the car she has calmed down. They drive to the heliport.*

**Scene 52.** EXT. HELIPORT. DAY

*Jan, Terry and Pits emerge from the changing rooms in their survival suits. They kiss Dodo and Bess on their way to the helicopter. Jan kisses Bess hard and long. Then he climbs aboard and the door shuts. The helicopter engines rev up. Suddenly Bess begins to scream. She tears herself away from Dodo. She shakes the door handle. She manages to get the door open. She hangs on to Jan and screams when Dodo tries to disengage her. Finally she has to let go, and the helicopter soars into the air. Dodo holds her on the landing pad.*

**Scene 53.** INT. HELICOPTER. DAY

*Jan looks down at her impotently. Once out above the sea he looks at Terry. Terry gives him a consoling grin.*

JAN Am I good enough for her?

TERRY Yes you are.

**Scene 54.** EXT. HELIPORT. DAY

*Ashore, Bess hiccups in Dodo's arms. Dodo forces a pill down her throat.*

DODO It's only four weeks ...

**Scene 55.** PANORAMA SCENE

*LS of heliport with helicopter rising. We are so high up that we can easily take in the fjord with more than a dozen oil rigs drawn up for repair. Day.*

**Scene 56.** INT. CHURCH. DAY

*Bess is kneeling.*

BESS (in her own voice) Dear Father in Heaven, I am so miserable ...

(in assumed gruff voice) You deserve to be.

(Frightened, in her own voice) Why do I deserve to be?

(Gruff voice) You are guilty of selfishness, Bess. You didn't consider even for a second how painful it must have been for him. You put your own feelings before anyone else's.

(In her own voice) But I love him so badly.

(Gruff voice) I can't see that you love him when you behave
like that. Now you must promise me you'll be a good girl.
(In her own voice) I promise to be a good girl.

### Scene 57. INT. CHURCH. VESTIBULE. DAY

*As Bess comes out of the church she meets her mother, who is washing
the floor of the vestibule.*

BESS I'm sorry for the way I behaved, Mother.

BESS'S MOTHER That's better, Bess my girl.

*Bess embraces her mother.*

BESS Mother, would it be OK if I came home for a bit while Jan's
away?

BESS Of course it would, Bessie.

### Scene 58. INT. BESS'S MOTHER'S HOUSE. EVENING

*Bess is listening to Radio Luxembourg. Her mother has dozed off with
her knitting in her lap. Dodo gets home. She takes off her coat. She is
in a nurse's uniform. She looks at Bess.*

BESS Have you taken my calendar?

DODO (in a whisper, so as not to wake mother) What would I
want your calendar for?

BESS You've taken it!

DODO Listen, you must stop ... worshipping him like this, it's not
good for you. You've got to live on the days he's not here too.
I mean, you're not dead just because he isn't here! It's sick to
believe you're dead just because you're on your own.

BESS Where is it?

*Dodo retrieves a cardboard calendar from the waste bin. Dodo gives Bess
the calendar. It's torn in half. Bess holds it for a moment. Then she begins
to cry tears of rage. She throws the calendar to the floor and runs out of
the room. Dodo picks it up and looks at it in despair. Four weeks have
been marked out in big black crosses and little drawings of teardrops.*

### Scene 59. PANORAMA SCENE

*LS from out at sea of Bess who is wandering around in the half
darkness just outside town, screaming out her rage at the water's edge.*

*The waves break against the shore. Night.*

**Scene 60.** EXT. RIG. NIGHT
*Jan is on the night shift. He, Terry and Pits are each in their overalls beside the drill. The work they're doing is filthy, hard and wet. Jan is panting.*

**Scene 61.** INT. RIG. SHOWERS. NIGHT
*After work Jan, Terry and Pits shower together and then go off to their cabins on the hotel platform.*

**Scene 62.** INT. RIG. JAN'S CABIN
*Jan looks at a photo of Bess before lying down to go to sleep.*

**Scene 63.** INT. TELEPHONE KIOSK BY CHURCH. DAY
*Bess is in the red telephone kiosk.*
BESS (to herself) Dear God, teach me to endure. Help me when he phones so I won't hurt him because I love him too much.
*Bess looks at her watch. It's a quarter to two. Dodo emerges from the church, carrying some shopping bags. She stops and looks at Bess.*
DODO (gravely) When is he meant to ring?
BESS A quarter past, but he might ring early ... by mistake.
*Dodo strokes her hair.*
DODO Shall I wait with you?
BESS Oh, yes, would you?

**Scene 64.** EXT. RIG. DAY
*Jan looks at his watch. It is ten past two. He, Terry and Pits are at work.*
JAN Where the hell is the next shift? My name's down for the radio telephone at a quarter past.
*Terry shrugs his shoulders. Jan works fiercely and looks thunderous.*

**Scene 65.** INT. TELEPHONE KIOSK BY CHURCH. DAY
*It is half past two by Bess's watch. Dodo looks at Bess in concern. Bess is shivering.*

DODO I have to get to work. Don't wait too long now, will you? Promise, now?

*Bess smiles and nods. Dodo leaves on her bike.*

**Scene 66.** INT. RIG. SHOWERS. DAY
*Jan is in the shower. He looks up at the clock. It is half past four. He hurries into his clothes.*

**Scene 67.** INT. RIG. RADIO ROOM. DAY
*Jan appears just as the radio operator is locking up. Jan grabs him.*

**Scene 68.** EXT./INT. TELEPHONE KIOSK BY CHURCH. NIGHT—INT. RIG. RADIO ROOM. NIGHT
*We see the church in the evening darkness. Bess is asleep in the telephone kiosk. Some time passes. Then the phone begins to ring. Bess doesn't wake up. It rings for a long time. Jan is seated at the radio on the rig, waiting impatiently. The phone falls silent. Bess is deep asleep. Jan sits impatiently. The radio operator looks at him interrogatively. Jan indicates that he should try again. The radio operator tries again. The phone rings in the telephone kiosk. The minister comes out of his house and answers it.*

JAN (impatiently, at other end of line) Bess—is Bess there?

*The minister bends towards Bess, who is sitting on the bottom of the kiosk, fast asleep. The minister rouses her.*

MINISTER There is a telephone call for you ...

*The minister retires.*

JAN Hallo ... Is that you ...

*Jan brightens into a smile. Bess rubs the sleep from her eyes.*

BESS (withdrawn, rather aloof) Hi.

JAN I'm sorry ... I couldn't get to the phone earlier ...

BESS That's OK.

JAN Is something up?

BESS No.

JAN (laughs) Don't you love me any more?

BESS (in fright) Of course I do.

JAN Say so then ...

BESS I'd made up my mind not to ...

*Jan looks up at the radio operator, who is standing there watching him. He grabs four packets of cigarettes from his pocket and gives them to the radio operator. The latter accepts the cigarettes, shrugs, and goes out.*

JAN Why not?

BESS I thought it might make you mad.

JAN Why should it make me mad?

BESS Everyone says I love you too much. If you found out how much I loved you you might get upset ... I mean because we're not together right now.

JAN Listen, Bess, you must never stop saying you love me. D'you hear?

BESS (faintly) Yes.

JAN No matter what anybody says.

BESS Yes.

JAN So say it.

BESS I love you.

JAN I love you too.

BESS (begins to cry) I love you so much.

*She cries a little. Then there is silence, and just the hiss of the phone line.*

BESS Are you there?

JAN Yes.

BESS I can hear you breathing. Can you hear me (breathing)?

JAN (listens, then:) Yes.

*Bess dries her eyes.*

JAN It is good that we can talk to each other ...

BESS (smiles)Yes.

JAN I don't know what to say ...

BESS (apologetically)Nor do I.

(frightened) You mustn't hang up.

JAN No, of course not ... We don't have to say anything ...

*They listen to each other's breathing. For a long time they work in silence at breathing together, and become almost hypnotised, only interrupted now and then by the crackle of the radio waves.*

**Scene 69.** INT. RIG. JAN'S CABIN. NIGHT

*Jan wakes up in his tiny cabin. It is the middle of the night. He lies there a moment, then lights a cigarette. He stares up at the ceiling.*

**Scene 70.** INT. BESS'S MOTHER'S HOUSE. BEDROOM. NIGHT

*Bess is lying awake in a double bed. Beside her, Dodo is fast asleep. Bess looks grave. She turns on the radio, very low. She listens to some distant beat music. She looks at the light from the radio on the wall. Then she smiles.*

**Scene 71.** INT. TELEPHONE KIOSK BY CHURCH. DAY—INT. RIG, RADIO ROOM. DAY

*Bess is in the telephone box with her eyes closed, breathing. The minister happens by. He watches her for a while, bemused, and then continues on his way. Jan is in the radio room. Outside the radio operator is smoking a cigarette. He watches Jan through a little window. Jan gets up and blocks the window with his back.*

JAN It works ... Don't you think it works?

BESS Yes, it works.

JAN Even though we're so far apart.

BESS (whispers) Yes.

JAN What are you thinking?

BESS (giggles) That you are here ...

JAN And what are you doing?

BESS I'm kissing you.

*Bess looks around to make sure she is unobserved.*

JAN I'm kissing you, too.

BESS It's good.

JAN Yes.

BESS (quietly) You can touch me if you like.

JAN I am touching you. I am touching your breasts.

*She smiles into the receiver.*

BESS I can feel it ... No, don't stop! I love you!

JAN Are you touching me?

BESS Yes. You're all sweaty ... aren't you?

JAN (smiles) I've been at work.

BESS You're so strong ... I'm touching your arms and your chest and your tummy and ...

JAN Say it!

BESS (almost inaudibly) ... your prick ...

(shocked at herself, she glances at the church, and then smiles) ... you're so huge ...

## Scene 72. PANORAMA SCENE

*LS of radio tower on the outermost little skerry. A storm is brewing. The clouds tower like a menacing wall. Day.*

## Scene 73. INT. SHOP. DAY

*Bess is washing the floor in the back of the shop wearing a smock. Dodo has been shopping. She is sitting on a box with some bags. Dodo look at Bess, who is quite mute.*

DODO It can't be long now?

BESS He will be back in ten days ... for a week.

*Pits suddenly appears in the shop. Bess sees him and runs to him.*

BESS Pits ... what are you doing ashore? Where's Jan?

*Bess is beside herself. Pits shows her his bandaged wrist.*

PITS I'm the only one back. Hurt my wrist.

BESS Oh.

*Bess almost cries from disappointment. Pits embraces both of them.*

PITS He sends his love.

## Scene 74. PANORAMA SCENE

*The oil rig at sea, a storm brewing. Evening.*

## Scene 75. INT. RIG. JAN'S CABIN. NIGHT

*Jan is resting in his cabin. The rain is lashing the porthole. He looks at the filthy weather indifferently. Terry comes in. He sits down on the bed.*

TERRY Sodding drill's stuck again. They say they want even more torque.

JAN More?!!

TERRY Well what the fuck—it's not the first time.

*Terry gets up.*

TERRY *See you at nine.*

JAN (firmly) After my call, not before. The drill will have to wait.

*Terry laughs.*

## Scene 76. INT. TELEPHONE KIOSK BY CHURCH. NIGHT

*Bess is holding the receiver.*

BESS (shouts into the receiver) I can't hear you!

JAN Bess ... Bess ...

*The line hums and crackles. Bess is tearful with disappointment.*

BESS Where are you Jan?

*The line goes dead.*

BESS Jan ... JAN!

*For ages, Bess listens for signs of life. She sobs, the receiver in her hand. The storm thunders in the sky above her.*

## Scene 77. PANORAMA SCENE

*LS of radio tower on outermost skerry. The storm is at its peak. The waves break high above the radio tower's metal legs. Evening.*

## Scene 78. EXT. CHURCH. NIGHT

*Bess knows where the key is  hidden, beneath a board. She retrieves it and quietly lets herself into the church.*

## Scene 79. INT. CHURCH. NIGHT

*Bess kneels. She makes to speak, but is unable to start. She tries again. She can't find the words.*

BESS (in the gruff voice) Yes, Bess? ... What is it you want?

(In her own voice) Father, I am so wretched ... I don't think I can endure it. I love him so badly.

(In the gruff voice) Bess McNiell, for many years you prayed for love. Shall I take it away from you again? Is that what you want?

(In her own voice) No, oh no! I'm still grateful for love.

(In the gruff voice) Well, what do you want then?

(In her own voice) I pray for Jan to come home.

(In the gruff voice) He will be coming home in ten days. You must learn to endure, you know that.

(In her own voice) I can't wait.

(In the gruff voice) This is unlike you, Bess. Out there, there are people who need Jan and his work. What about them?

(In her own voice, desperately) They don't matter. Nothing else matters. I just want Jan home again. I pray to you! Oh, please won't you send him home?

(In the gruff voice) Are you sure that's what you want, Bess?

(In her own voice) Yes.

*Bess looks resolutely up into the darkness of the ceiling. Silence.*


**Scene 80**. EXT. RIG. NIGHT

*Jan trots as he tugs on his overalls. He meets Terry, who has already started work. Somebody bawled at Jan for being late. Terry smiles at him. The drill is noisy. They extend the drill in a cloud of oily water. They drill again. The drill slows down. It is labouring hard. Everyone steps back, except Terry.*

JAN Terry!

*Jan calls him, but Terry can't hear him.*

JAN TERRY!

*Jan gets through to him. He waves him back. As Terry turns towards Jan the drill explodes. A cloud of oil covers everything. Oil spouts from the hole. Everyone runs for cover. Jan looks around.*

JAN TERRY! TERRY!

*Terry has disappeared in the sea of oil. Jan spots him. He struggles through the spray towards him. A long length of drill is lying across him. Jan shakes at the drill. With almost inhuman strength Jan manages to lift the length of drill. A couple of men haul Terry to safety. Terry's eyes open. He sends Jan a smile. Jan responds with a beaming smile of his own, relieved because his friend is in safety. At that instant a second oil explosion enshrouds Jan, who is slung back into the oil, mud and water and disappears.*


**Scene 81.** INT. BESS'S MOTHER'S HOUSE. BEDROOM. NIGHT

*Bess wakes up. She looks around. Dodo is asleep. Bess tries to find a*

*station on the radio, but it's no good. She turns the radio off. She gazes out into the storm.*

## Scene 82. INT. BESS'S MOTHER'S HOUSE. DAY

*Bess is clearing away the breakfast things. The doorbell rings. Bess's mother opens the door. Bess comes out behind her. The minister is standing on the doorstep.*

MINISTER (sotto voce, rapidly) It's Jan ... there's been an accident on the rig.

*Bess stares at him for a moment in confusion, and then she faints.*

## Scene 83. EXT. HELIPORT. DAY

*Bess is waiting at the heliport with the ambulance crew, Dodo in uniform, and Dr. Richardson. The waves are almost breaking over the landing pad. The helicopter lands. Wordlessly, as quick as a flash, Dr. Richardson and Dodo are helped aboard. The rotors keep turning. Bess watches as the doctor examines Jan's head. It is bandaged. The people on the helicopter talk, but their words are inaudible. Dr. Richardson climbs down. He goes up to Bess.*

DR. RICHARDSON We can't do anything for him here ... He'll have to go to Glasgow. We'll fly him on.

*Bess looks horror-stricken. Dr. Richardson looks at her and then he smiles.*

DR. RICHARDSON Come along!

*He takes Bess by the hand and leads her aboard the helicopter. He positions her on a seat beside Dodo, just across from Jan's stretcher. He says something unintelligible to the pilot. The door closes and the helicopter takes off instantly.*

## Scene 84. INT. HELICOPTER. DAY

*Jan's eyes are closed. His hands are crossed on his chest.*

BESS (leans right over him) Jan, can you hear me?

*Jan smiles, his eyes closed, half-hidden by the bandages.*

JAN Yes ...

*Bess smiles. He reaches for his hand. Jan senses her movement.*

JAN Don't touch my hands ...

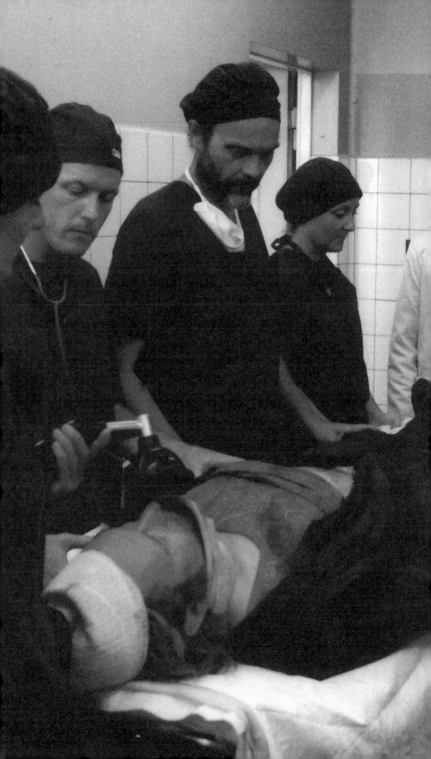

*Bess has already taken one of them, but lets it drop, shaken. It flops down beside the stretcher.*

JAN I said no!

*Jan is angry in a way she has never heard before.*

JAN (angrily) So do as you're told!

*Bess jerks away from him in fright. Dodo looks at her. She picks up Jan's hand and puts it back on his chest. She touches Bess, but Bess pulls away. Jan's face twists in pain. Dr. Richardson gives him an injection.*

Scene 85. INT. HOSPITAL. CORRIDORS. DAY

*Jan is wheeled rapidly through Casualty to Surgery. Dodo follows, holding Bess by the hand. Jan is strapped onto a machine and lifted into the air for a CAT scan. Dr. Richardson is talking to another doctor. Jan is unconscious now. They try to rouse him, but in vain. Bess covers her face with her hands. They inject a contrast medium to displace the cerebrospinal fluid. Dodo leads Bess outside.*

Scene 86. INT. HOSPITAL. GLASGOW. SURGERY. DAY

*Dodo and Bess sit wordlessly for a while. Dr. Richardson comes out.*

DR. RICHARDSON They're going to operate straight away.

*A porter and a nurse wheel Jan away towards the sterile area. Bess runs after them. She clutches the trolley and runs along beside it. Dodo comes up. Bess looks at her sternly.*

BESS I want to go with him!

*Dodo shakes her head.*

DODO You can't.

BESS I want to go with him!

DODO Bess, it'll be too much for you.

*Bess won't give an inch.*

Scene 87. INT. HOSPITAL. GLASGOW. SCRUBBING UP ROOM. DAY

*Dodo helps Bess into a gown and mask. Dodo gets changed for the operation too.*

**Scene 88**. INT. HOSPITAL. GLASGOW. OPERATING THEATRE.
NIGHT

*Jan has been strapped into a grotesque position on the operating table.
He comes round for a brief instant before the anaesthetic is administered. Firstly he looks up at Bess, almost beseechingly. Then he smiles
a soothing smile. The anaesthetic is administered and he's prepared
for the operation.*

DODO (whispers) You'd better go outside now.

*Bess shakes her head. Dodo talks to a doctor in a low voice. She nods
to Bess that she may stay. Bess watches as they operate on Jan's head.
Dodo puts Bess's hand in his. The doctors work quietly. Every machine
and movement makes Bess jump. It looks very dramatic now they are
inside Jan's skull.*

**Scene 89.** INT. HOSPITAL. GLASGOW. OPERATING THEATRE.
NIGHT

*When the time comes to close Jan's head up, Dodo leads Bess away.*

DODO You are awfully brave ...

*Bess looks gravely at Dodo.*

BESS I want you to pray with me.

*Dodo looks around in embarrassment when Bess kneels down on the
operating theatre floor. They pray together. Bess speaks the words.*

BESS Dear God, we pray that you will hold your hand over Jan,
and not let him die ...

**Scene 90.** INT. HOSPITAL. GLASGOW. CORRIDOR. OFFICE.
DAY

*Bess is waiting in the corridor outside the doctor's office. She is called
in by a nurse. The doctor is at his desk. He is immersed in Jan's file.
Dr. Richardson is also present. He gives Bess a soothing smile.*

DOCTOR Do sit down.

*Bess sits down.*

BESS Will he live?

DOCTOR We have stabilised your husband's condition for the
time being.

BESS (glancing at Dr. Richardson) Will he live?

61

DR. RICHARDSON (smiles) Yes, Bess, he will live.

BESS (smiles) That's the important thing.

DOCTOR I'm not so sure. Your husband suffered serious injuries. The lesions in his brain are extensive. Life shouldn't always be preserved at any cost.

BESS What do you mean?

DR. RICHARDSON The doctor means that if life isn't worth living, it may be better to die.

BESS (confused, to Dr. Richardson) Better to die? You don't know Jan. Or you couldn't say such a thing.

DOCTOR Your husband may never walk again. We think he will be completely paralysed.

BESS But he'll live.

DOCTOR Yes, he'll live, it seems.


Scene 91. INT. HOSPITAL. GLASGOW. WARD. EVENING

*Cautiously, Bess enters the white room where Jan is lying in bed. It is quiet, despite all the pipes and instruments. Jan's eyes are closed. She moves up quietly beside him.*

BESS (whispers) Jan my love ...

JAN (feebly, his eyes still shut) Not now ...

*Bess sits down on a chair and watches him fall asleep.*


Scene 92. INT. CAFETERIA. GLASGOW. EVENING

*Bess is sitting on her own with a plate of fish and chips lying untouched in front of her. She looks at some decoration with electric light completely in her own thoughts. She is tired. She wakes up and looks around the empty cafeteria. She clasps her hands and closes her eyes.*

BESS Father in Heaven, are you there? Are you still there?

(Gruff voice) Of course I am, Bess, you know that.

(Her voice) What is happening?

(Gruff voice) You wanted Jan home.

(Her voice) I've changed my mind! Why did I ask for that?

(Gruff voice) Because you are a stupid little girl Bess. Anyway I had to test you. Your love for Jan has been put to the test.

(Her voice) Thank you for not letting him die.

(Gruff voice) You're welcome, Bess.

**Scene 93.** PANORAMA SCENE

*Skyline of rainy evening over Glasgow. The rain glides across the frame. The last of the sun forms a faint rainbow. Evening.*

**Scene 94.** INT. CHURCH. DAY

*The minister is walking around the packed church. Suddenly he turns towards a man sitting in one of the pews. He points at him. The man gets to his feet and prays in very rapid Gaelic. The minister proceeds to another man and starts him off. And another. Bess is sitting beside Grand-father William. The minister sets William off. Bess looks at him as he prays.*


**Scene 95.** INT. CHURCH. VESTIBULE. DAY

*Bess and her grand-father leave the church.*

**BESS** It's stupid only letting men do the praying during services. I bet God never said that.

**WILLIAM** (whispers sharply) Hold your tongue, woman!

*Bess shuts up and looks down. Sybilla comes up to them.*

**SYBILLA** Hallo Bess, when did you get back?

**BESS** (smiles) I came back with Jan. He's over at the hospital now.


**Scene 96.** INT. HOSPITAL. JAN'S ROOM. DAY

*Bess is sitting beside Jan in his room at the local hospital. He is awake. She is in the T-shirt and short dress he gave her. She is holding his hand. Terry comes in with Pits. They smile.*

**TERRY** Hi there, champ!

**JAN** (smiling) Hello guys ... did you find anything?

**TERRY** A bit of gas, nothing really. Now guess what? We're heading north!

**JAN** North is good.

**TERRY** (with a big smile) You always said that's where the oil was.

**PITS** What are you doing here anyway? We're meant to be out drilling!

**JAN** I just need to keep my feet up for a bit, and then I'll be with you again. Just you wait!

*Everyone laughs. Bess beams at her husband. Pits opens a few cans of beer. He passes one to Terry and puts one on the table for Jan. He raises his can to Jan.*

PITS Bottoms up then Jan.

*Jan shakes his head feebly.*

*Terry whispers to Pits. Pits looks at Jan's arms.*

PITS (embarrassed) Sorry mate ...

JAN Forget it. I wasn't thirsty anyway.

*Terry look at Jan for a while.*

TERRY (breakes into a smile) Sure!

*Terry takes the bottle and hold it to Jans lips.*

TERRY Here you go ...

*Jan drinks. Bess look at it with a smile. Jan starts to cough. Terry takes the bottle away. Terry and Pits stand there a little while.*

TERRY Be seeing you, Jan.

PITS Yes. Cheers Jan, get well soon!

*They leave. Jan watches them with a smile. Then he looks at Bess. His face stiffens. He turns serious.*

JAN (quietly) I want to you to do something for me.

BESS (sits down again and smiles) Yes?

JAN It's just that ... when you come here, could you wear a loose blouse and a long dress? Please. Would you mind?

*He looks at her beseechingly. She sits there in silence. He looks at her breasts beneath the tight T-shirt, then at her legs. He looks for a long time. His eyes caress her. Neither of them moves. Finally it becomes too painful for him. Great tears begin running down his cheeks as he looks. Dodo enters.*

DODO Right, I'll just give you something to help you rest ...

*She ignores his tears, and gives him an injection.*

DODO And now you must go, Bess. Jan needs to rest.

*Dodo leads Bess out firmly.*

**Scene 97.** INT. HOSPITAL. CORRIDOR. NURSES' STATION. DAY

*In the corridor Dodo is angry. She tugs Bess along behind her. She pulls her into an office.*

**DODO** The stupidest thing you can do is sit here bawling your eyes out with him. If you can't cheer him up, you'll just have to stay away!

**BESS** (quietly) I am sorry.

*Bess stands there for a while, ashamed.*

**BESS** Is he asleep now?

**DODO** Yes, unless you got him too excited ...

*Dodo is still angry. Bess looks at her beseechingly.*

**BESS** I don't s'pose it'd hurt if I went in and looked at him while he's asleep, would it?

*Dodo smiles.*

**DODO** Go on then ... With what I've given him he won't be that easy to rouse ...

*Dodo gives Bess a hug.*


**Scene 98**. INT. HOSPITAL. JAN'S ROOM. DAY

*Bess is standing beside Jan's bed. She caresses his slumbering body, kisses his face ... carefully, so as not to wake him.*

**BESS** I love you Jan.

(In a deep voice) I love you too Bess, you are the love of my life.

(In her own voice) I want to help you so dreadfully.

(In a deep voice) I know you do, Bess. You help me by being strong.


**Scene 99**. INT. BESS'S MOTHER'S HOUSE. BEDROOM. NIGHT

*Dodo is lying awake in the double bed. She switches the light on when Bess comes in.*

**DODO** Where have you been?

**BESS** For a walk.

**DODO** Till 2 in the morning?

*Bess goes out and returns in her nightie.*

**DODO** For goodness sake talk to me! ... You used to tell me every thing!

*She gets into bed with her back to Dodo and closes her eyes. Dodo sits up a bit.*

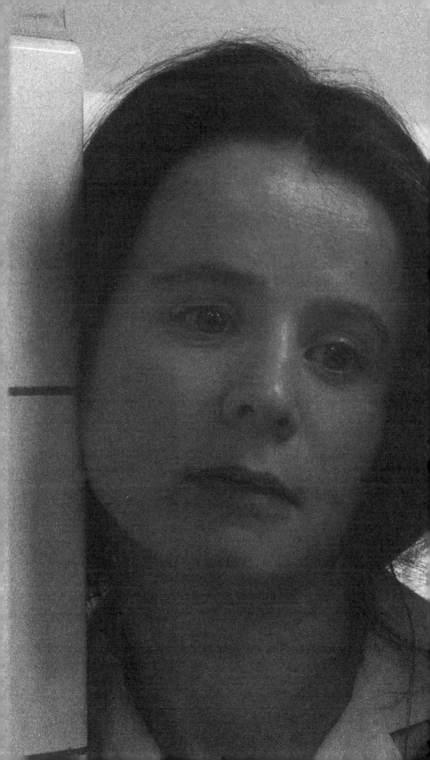

DODO Listen ... I don't want you getting ill again like you did when Sam died.

BESS I've been to the church.

DODO You heard me, I don't want you getting ill again like you did when Sam died. This isn't a church matter ... I've talked to Dr. Richardson. He can see you tomorrow.

*Bess pulls the covers right up.*

BESS (coldly) Can he.

DODO Will you go?

BESS OK. May I go to sleep now?

*Dodo turns off the light but doesn't go to sleep. Bess pulls the covers even higher.*

BESS Why do you always talk to me as if I was a wee bairn?

**Scene 100**. INT. HOSPITAL. CORRIDOR. DAY

*Bess is sitting on a chair outside an office. She is kicking the leg of the chair thoughtfully. Interestedly she watches the shadows cast by bushes beyond the window. A nurse comes out and shows Bess in.*

**Scene 101**. INT. HOSPITAL. DR. RICHARDSON'S OFFICE. DAY

*Dr. Richardson is sitting at his desk. Bess sits down on a chair on the other side of the desk. They sit in silence for a while. Then she begins to cry. He comes round the desk to her with a handkerchief. He sits down on the desk and looks at her.*

BESS Dodo said I had to come.

DR. RICHARDSON I know ... she has this idea about me treating you.

(Looks at her file) My predecessor admitted you a few years ago, I can see. Why did he do that?

BESS I don't know.

DR. RICHARDSON No, nor do I. You were upset because your brother had died, and now you are upset because your husband is ill. Nothing unusual about that.

BESS Aren't I going to have some pills?

DR. RICHARDSON I'm probably not like your old doctor. I don't think people should be given pills because they do what's only natural. When we hurt ourselves we say 'ouch', and if we're sad we cry. You're a sensitive little thing. Maybe showing what you feel isn't quite the done thing where you come from, but it's certainly no disease.

BESS I wouldn't have come by myself ...

DR. RICHARDSON You can go again too, if you want.

*He looks at her calmly. She begins to cry again.*

BESS I love him so much, but it's like the more I love him the more I hurt him.

DR. RICHARDSON What do you mean?

BESS I just want to be together with the man I love, is that a crime?

DR. RICHARDSON Not at all.

BESS Why does it have to be so difficult?

DR. RICHARDSON Tell me how you hurt your husband.

BESS It was my fault.

DR. RICHARDSON You'll have to explain.

BESS What happened on the rig was my fault.

DR. RICHARDSON How come?

BESS I prayed to God to send him home to me ...

*Dr. Richardson smiles.*

DR. RICHARDSON Goodness what powers you possess ... do you really believe you possess such powers? I know you people believe a lot about yourselves. Perhaps you should do a bit of grieving for yourself instead of for him. After all, it's pretty tough luck on you too, eh?

*He puts his arm round her shoulders.*

DR. RICHARDSON You have a great deal to endure alone ... as I told Dodo, I'd like to help you, but you must come of your own accord, not because she makes you ...

*Bess nods.*

DR. RICHARDSON I think you should come and see me now and then if you feel like it—and if you feel like a little chat ... or just feel like sitting ... if there is anything you feel I can do ...

BESS Thank you.

*She begins to cry again.*

BESS I'm sorry.

DR. RICHARDSON (putting a hand on her shoulder) I expect things'll look up once you get him home again.

*(Suggested music: 'Barbara O'Reilly', The Who. Underlies the following scenes. Concludes on Panorama scene: icicles in foreground).*

**Scene 102.** PANORAMA SCENE

*Mountains in winter. Thick snow is falling. Day.*

**Scene 102.** INT./EXT. MONTAGE: HOSPITAL/BESS'S MOTHER'S HOUSE/RIG/SUNDRY/DAY/NIGHT

*Winter montage. Jan is lying in hospital, Bess often there beside him. Bess is washing the floors in the shop. The rig is being moved. Oil being found in the howling blizzard. Terry and Pits jubilant as the new oil spurts over them. Terry takes his helmet off and lets the oil spurt over his head. He puts his oily fingers on the camera lens. Jan being taken home to the little bedroom with sloping walls that Dodo and Bess have got ready upstairs in Bess's mother's house. Jan being nursed by Bess and Dodo. Dodo gives Jan a sleeping pill every evening from the jar on the dresser. Bess clowns about for Jan. Sometimes he responds, sometimes not. Bess is fascinated by the reflection of some light in Jan's glass of water, projected onto the wallpaper.*

**Scene 103.** PANORAMA SCENE

*Icicles in foreground of the big waterfall out by the coast. The thaw has set in. Day.*

**Scene 104.** INT. BESS'S MOTHER'S HOUSE. JAN'S ROOM. DAY

*It is Jan's birthday. Bess has laid his tray beautifully. Dodo gives him his tea from a cup with a nipple. Bess opens her present to him. It's a mechanical toy. A little fat man who keeps falling over and looking surprised. Bess demonstrates it on the tray. Dodo and Bess laugh each time it falls over. Bess laughs so much she has tears in her eyes. Dodo notices that Jan is looking at nothing but Bess. She pats Bess on the*

70

*head and puts her coat on over her nurse's uniform. She goes out. Bess is still laughing in delight every time he falls. Now she looks at Jan, who is grave.*

**BESS** Don't you think it's funny?

**JAN** (in a low voice) Shut the door, will you.

*Bess looks at him beseechingly, but she gets up and closes the door.*

**JAN** I'm trying to imagine what I would do in your shoes.

**BESS** (quietly) Jan, not now ...

**JAN** Bess, I know I couldn't live with such a marriage, not with my wife being a ... living dead. I know that I'm not that good a man. For God's sake, the world is full of men who can move their arms and legs.

*Bess shakes her head.*

**BESS** Jan ...

**JAN** Let me talk! I've thought about this hard. The trouble is that the people in this fucking prison would slowly but surely kill you if you divorced me.

**BESS** Jan!

**JAN** Let me finish. It's bad enough having to lie here like this. I don't want to go through the torment of suffocating you too. I've never met anyone like you Bess. I really haven't. What the hell made me ever go off and leave you?

*Bess's eyes are brimming with tears.*

**JAN** Listen, I want you to think about what I'm going to say. Real ly think about it ... I want you to take a lover, Bess. You can do that without anybody finding out.

*His words are like a physical blow to Bess. She struggles for breath.*

**BESS** Do you think so little of me? Do you think that's what I want? Oh, you stupid, stupid man ...

*Bess is as if turned to stone. Then the anger comes.*

**BESS** You ... you ... cripple!

*She just has to get out. She runs down the stairs.*

**Scene 105.** EXT. STREET. DAY

*Bess runs down the street.*

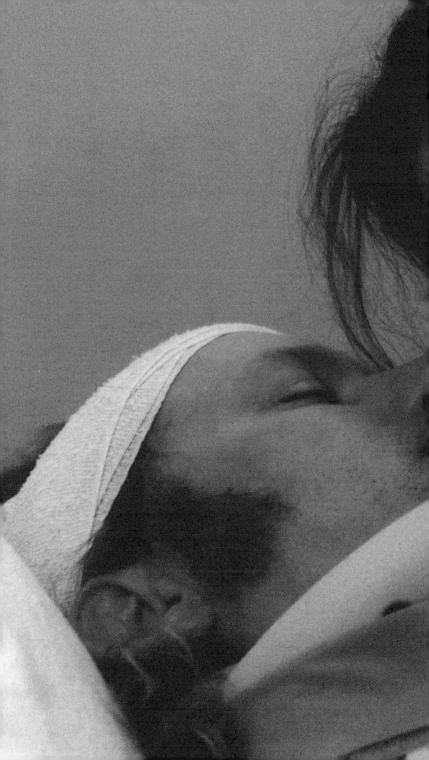

**Scene 106**. EXT. CEMETERY. DAY

*Bess wanders up and down the paths in the cemetery until she has calmed down.*

**Scene 107**. INT. CHURCH. DAY

*Bess is on her way into the church to pray. The minister appears from inside. She looks at him miserably. He puts an arm round her shoulders and leads her into his house.*

**Scene 108**. INT. MINISTER'S HOUSE. DAY

*Bess and the minister are sitting on opposite sides of the desk. The minister is talking to Bess in a low voice.*

MINISTER You must make up with him. A husband and wife have to be able to talk to each other. He's the one who's help-less, and you're the one who must show you're strong. Go to him and tell him you are sorry you were angry. You have God. You have the strength that your life in God has bestowed upon you, and that is a strength he does not possess.

**Scene 109**. EXT. MARKET. NIGHT

*The stalls are closing. Bess runs up. She wants to buy some flowers. Only the very best will do. The stall-holder smiles at her child-like joy and impatience.*

**Scene 110**. INT. BESS'S MOTHER'S HOUSE. JAN'S ROOM. NIGHT

*Jan is looking at the pill jar on the dresser. He can reach the little table cloth. Infinitely slowly, with the only two fingers he can move, he pulls the jar to the edge of the dresser. He lies there for a while, regaining his strength. Then he goes for it. He tugs the cloth. By pressing it against the side of the dresser with is two fingers, he can just stop the jar from falling to the floor. He manoeuvres the jar into his hand and slowly eases the lid off. He drops some of the pills, but he empties the re-mainder onto his bedspread. Using his mouth, he manages to raise the bedspread with the pills towards his face, centimetre by centimetre. Dodo enters. She looks at Jan. Then she picks up the pills and puts them back into the jar. She drops the jar into her apron pocket. Jan closes his eyes. Then he begins to cry. She looks at him. He sobs violently. She puts her arms round him ad holds him tight. Slowly he calms down. She gets up. Then she notices the tray and the mechanical toy.*

DODO (angrily) Where is Bess? Have you been on your own all day?

JAN I scared her away.

DODO What is she thinking of? Leaving you to lie here like this ...

JAN Help me.

DODO If you mean the pills, forget it.

JAN (shakes his head) You were right. I was a danger to her ...

DODO No need to talk about that now.

JAN (smiles) Oh, there's every need. Whatever you might think, she was happy when we wed. I'm not saying I made her happy, but I'm saying that the love did. She experienced love, and it became important for her life. She had the right to love ... like everybody. You must admit she blossomed ...

DODO (shrugs her shoulders) Maybe.

JAN I can't lie here and see her wither again. You must help me to set her free from me. She's not the one who got hit on the head by a length of drill. She must get out into the open air. She must get on with her life.

*Dodo looks at Jan for a long time.*

JAN Will you help me?

DODO What do you want me to do?

JAN Tell me how to make her realise that all I want is for her to go on living.

DODO (thinks) She'd do anything for you, Jan. She couldn't care less about herself. Thats how she is. She'd do anything for you, not for herself. She'd do anything for a smile from you.

*Jan lies there a moment. Then he smiles.*

JAN You're right. Thank you for telling me.

DODO (smiles) No trouble.

*Dodo begins to put things onto the tray. Jan gazes at the ceiling. His*

*breathing is laborious. She looks at him. He gasps for breath.*
DODO Are you all right?
JAN (in a daze) I'm slipping away again.
DODO Did you take any of those pills?
JAN No, no.
*Dodo gets out her stethoscope and listens to his chest.*

**Scene 111.** INT. BESS'S MOTHER'S HOUSE. NIGHT
*Bess runs in with the flowers. Her mother is in the kitchen. Bess runs on up the stairs without stopping. She sees the empty bed. Her mother comes up the stairs.*
BESS They took him back to hospital.

**Scene 112.** INT. HOSPITAL. CORRIDORS. NIGHT
*Bess runs along the corridors with the flowers.*

**Scene 113.** INT. HOSPITAL. CORRIDORS. NIGHT
*Dodo emerges from Jan's room just as Bess comes up. Dodo stops her.*
BESS I want to see him!
DODO Bess, what's all this about?
BESS What's happened?
DODO He went off ... Anyway it's no good having him at home any more.
(Angry now) Not when you just leave him like that. The man's completely helpless! Don't you see?
*Bess looks at Dodo beseechingly.*
BESS I'm sorry.
DODO That's not good enough.
BESS I'm not even allowed to kiss him any more. He has so much love in him, I know he has, but I'm not even allowed to kiss him ...
DODO Try listening to what he says instead. If you don't listen to him, he may just get so sick of everything that he won't want to live any more. You can do more for him than the doctors, Bess.

**Scene 114.** INT. HOSPITAL. JAN'S ROOM. NIGHT

*Bess is holding the flowers. She watches Dodo set up some drips. Jan looks staked out with drips and tubes. Dodo gives him an injection. Dodo goes out.*

BESS Jan?

JAN (with difficulty) Yes, sweetie.

BESS Sorry.

JAN (feebly) I am terribly tired, but there's something I have to say to you.

*Bess comes right up to his bedside and listens.*

JAN I lied to you. I'm sorry.

BESS (strokes his forehead) You're forgiven.

JAN (shakes his head) Bess, I don't want to die. I believe that love is a mighty power. If I die it will be because love cannot keep me alive. I lied when I told you that you should take a lover for your sake. It was for my sake, Bess. Because I don't want to die. Do you understand?

BESS No. I love you.

JAN I lie here, I can't do a thing ... You're there, Bess, of course you are, and I'm sure your love has kept me alive so far, but ... I can hardly remember what it's like to make love ... and if I forget what that's like, I'll die.

BESS I will always love you.

JAN Remember when I phoned you from the rig? The way we made love without being together?

BESS You want me to talk to you about that again? I'd love to.

JAN I want you to find a man to make love to. Then I want you to come back here to my bedside and tell me all about it. Then I'll feel it as if it was you and me together. That is what will keep me alive.

*He looks at her intensely.*

BESS (stands there for ages, in chok) I can't ...

*Jan dozes.*

JAN I lied to you this morning. You must love for me ... if you love me ... it is for me ... not for you ... it is for me, Bess ...

*Bess looks at him as he sleeps.*

**Scene 115**. INT. HOSPITAL. STAIRCASE. DAY

*Bess is walking down the stairs, lost in thought. She is still carrying the flowers. Suddenly she feels ill. She stops. She stands for a while with her eyes closed, swaying. Then she drops the flowers. Just as she is about to topple a hand grabs her. She looks up in confusion and gratitude. Dr. Richardson picks up the flowers and gives them back to her.*

**DR. RICHARDSON** Feeling better?

*Bess nods eagerly and he lets go. Almost at once she starts to fall over again, and he has to grab her.*


**Scene 116.** INT. HOSPITAL. DR. RICHARDSON'S OFFICE. NIGHT

*Bess is lying on the settee. She has a blanket over her. She is asleep. She wakes up. Dr. Richardson is talking to a nurse by the desk. He looks up and smiles.*

**DR. RICHARDSON** Well, you certainly needed some shut-eye.

*The nurse smiles and goes out. Dr. Richardson goes on working at his desk. Bess tries to get up.*

**DR. RICHARDSON** No, stay there ... I put your flowers in a vase.

*She looks at the flowers, which are still in paper, now in a hospital vase. Dr. Richardson looks up at Bess again.*

**DR. RICHARDSON** Worrying all the time is not good for anyone ... You should think of yourself a bit, too ... Go out, I mean ... Go dancing. I have seen you dance.

(smiles) You like to dance.

*Bess looks at Dr. Richardson. He smiles, but she averts his eyes bashfully.*

*(Suggested music: 'Cross-eyed Mary', Jethro Tull. )*


**Scene 117**. INT. HOSPITAL. JAN'S ROOM. NIGHT

*Terry is sitting by Jans bed drinking a beer.*

**JAN** I asked Bess to find a lover.

*Terry nods.*

**JAN** But she would never do that you know ... it's her religion. She is not like that. So today I told her to do it for me. I told her to go out and have sex with somebody else and then to come here and tell me about it. I told her that this way she could save my life. That hearing about the sex she had, would keep my sexuality alive. That I could not live without it.

*Terry sits for a while. He smiles.*

JAN She would never have another love in her life, with me lying here, if I had not told her that it was for me. She loves me so much. I set her free this way. By telling her that she could save my life. She deserves love.

TERRY Yes she deserves it.

JAN She will come here and tell me everything ...

TERRY Second thoughts?

JAN I love her ... it will hurt me to listen to what she has done with some other guy ...

TERRY (serious) I don't know what has happened to you since you got married. You sound like some god-damned priest. If she deserves to be screwed by some bloke, then you should be man enough to listen. It might even do you good, as you said.

JAN (laughs) Yeah, you're right.


**Scene 118.** INT. HOSPITAL. CORRIDOR. DAY

*Bess approaches along the corridor. She spends some time plucking up courage before she opens the door into Jan's room. She has brought the flowers again. Now she is ready. She enters.*


**Scene 119.** INT. HOSPITAL. JAN'S ROOM. DAY

*The room is empty. The bed has gone.*


**Scene 120.** INT. HOSPITAL. CORRIDOR. DAY

*Bess runs down to the nursing station.*


**Scene 121.** INT. HOSPITAL. NURSING STATION. DAY

*A young nurse is sitting at the nursing station.*

BESS Where's Jan?

YOUNG NURSE They took him to intensive care.

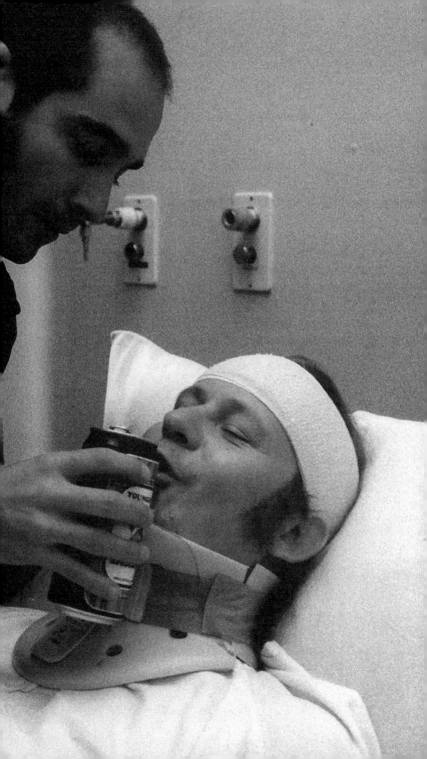

**Scene 122.** INT. HOSPITAL. CORRIDORS. DAY
*Bess runs through the hospital.*

**Scene 123.** INT. HOSPITAL. INTENSIVE CARE. DAY
*Dodo and a doctor are working on Jan who is unconscious. They are getting a respirator ready, ventilating him manually at the same time. Bess goes up to him. He can't see her. She looks at Dodo beseechingly. The doctor gets ready to cut a small hole in Jans neck for the tube.*
**DODO** Go outside, Bess. There is nothing you can do here now.
*Bess goes outside. With her flowers.*

**Scene 124.** EXT. COUNTRYSIDE. DAY
*Bess rides through the countryside on her moped.*

**Scene 125.** INT. CHURCH. DAY
*Bess is kneeling. She is looking at the daylight coming in through a window. She looks at the light changing.*
**BESS** Dear Father in Heaven don't let him die.
(The gruff voice) And why shouldn't I let him die?
(Her own voice) I love him.
(The gruff voice) So you keep saying. But I don't see it.
(Her own voice) There's nothing I can do. Nothing at all.
(The gruff voice) Prove to me that you love him, then I'll let him live.

**Scene 126.** INT. DR. RICHARDSON'S FLAT. LANDING OUT-SIDE. NIGHT
*Bess is standing on the landing outside the flat, holding the flowers and a bag. She rings the doorbell. He answers the door. He looks at her in surprise. She goes inside.*

**Scene 127.** INT. DR. RICHARDSON'S FLAT. NIGHT
*They enter. She looks round the flat. She gives him the flowers and gets a bottle of Scotch out of the bag. She puts it on the table. She looks at him.*

BESS I've come to dance.

*He smiles a touch ironically. She goes past him and puts a record on the recordplayer.*

## Scene 128. INT. MONTAGE. DR. RICHARDSONS' FLAT. NIGHT

*Dr. Richardson is sitting down. She is dancing. He looks at her with a smile.*

DR. RICHARDSON OK Bess, do you have something to say to me?

*Bess dances while shaking her head with a little smile.*

DR. RICHARDSON Would you like to tell me how you are, Bess?

*Bess pours two glasses from the bottle. She offers one to Dr. Richardson.*

BESS Cheers!

*Dr. Richardson takes the glass but does not drink. He puts down the glass.*

DR. RICHARDSON (serious) Bess talk to me.

BESS (smiling, as she goes into the bedroom) Give me a moment, then you can come in.

*She closes the door behind her.*

DR. RICHARDSON Bess ...

*Dr. Richardson looks at the closed door a little troubled.*

## Scene 129. INT. DR. RICHARDSON'S FLAT. BEDROOM. NIGHT

*Dr. Richardson opens the door to the bedroom. He looks in. Bess is lying naked on the top of the bed. Dr. Richardson shakes his head.*

BESS (whispering) You can touch me now ...

DR. RICHARDSON (severely) Bess, put your clothes on!

BESS No you don't understand. You can have me now.

DR. RICHARDSON Bess, listen. We are not going to make love. Put your clothes back on.

BESS (sorry) Why don't you want me? Don't you like me. You said that you liked me.

DR. RICHARDSON I like you Bess. Now put your clothes on.

*He picks up her clothes. She starts crying.*

BESS But you said that I could come to you. I will be good to you. I want us to make love.

**DR. RICHARDSON** If you have anything to talk to me about, we can meet at the hospital. All right?

**BESS** I don't want to talk ... don't you understand that I don't want to talk!

**DR. RICHARDSON** As you like, but put your clothes on now and go home. Bess, please!

*Bess pulls the blanket over her head and cries violently.*

## Scene 130. PANORAMA SCENE

*The whole coast, from far away and high up, from out at sea. The coast is bathed in fat rays of sunlight. Day.*

## Scene 131. PANORAMA SCENE

*From high up, down towards the billowing sea of clouds. Here and there gaps appear. Now we can clearly see the town far below through a gap in the bulging clouds. Day.*

## Scene 132. INT. HOSPITAL. INTENSIVE CARE. DAY

*Bess is sitting beside Jan. He is on a respirator but awake. He looks terrible. He has a drip.*

**BESS** (can hardly get the words out) I am lying ... on my back ... all naked ... he comes in and sees me ...

*Jan looks at her in silence. He gives her a faint smile as she comes to a halt. He smiles encouragingly.*

**BESS** He comes to me ... he kisses my breasts.

*Bess speaks very slowly, in a very low voice. Jan looks at her.*

**BESS** He enters me.

(She pulls herself together) He is pressing my legs over backwards. He is making love to me ... gently ...

*They are silent for a long time. Jan closes his eyes.*

**BESS** He is coming ...

*There is a long silence. Jan wakes up. He points at the pad on the table. Bess gives it to him, along with a ball-point. Laboriously, Jan writes: 'Who?'*

**BESS** (on the verge of tears) Dr. Richardson.

*Jan smiles. He takes her hand. He writes again: 'You made it up.'*

84

**Bess** I tried. I really did.

*Bess runs out of the room.*


**Scene 133**. INT. HOSPITAL. JAN'S ROOM. NIGHT

*Dr. Richardson stands by Jans bed. Jan is in the respirator. Dodo is there too.*

**Dr. Richardson** You feel so bad because some fluid has built up in your head. We have decided to give you some medicin to make you sleep. That may make the pressure go down a bit and you will feel better. We will keep you asleep for a couple of days ... then we'll see how you are.

*Dodo administers the injection into the drop.*


**Scene 134.** INT. HOSPITAL. JAN'S ROOM. DAY

*Bess is sitting by Jans bed. He is asleep. The respirator is working. His body is jerking a little now and then. His face is twisting as in pain. Bess looks at him tormented. Dodo comes in. She gives him some more medicin in the drop.*

**Bess** Must you give him that?

*Dodo smiles.*

**Bess** Is he dreaming do you think?

**Dodo** He might be.

**Bess** I don't think it is a nice dream.


**Scene 135.** INT. HOSPITAL. JAN'S ROOM. DAY

*Bess is sitting down. She looks anxious. Jan is half awake again. Dr. Richardson and Dodo come in and examine him. Jan looks poorly and doped. Dr. Richardson stands with Dodo.*

**Dr. Richardson** We are going to take you of the respirator for five minuttes to exercise your lungs a little bit and to see how you are ...

*Dodo helps Dr.Richardson to remove the tube. They put a kind of a bandage over the hole. Jan is doing his best contolling his lungs on his own. Bess suffers with him as he is working. She comes close to him as Dr. Richardson is checking Jan's bloodpressure. Jan is breathing laboriously now.*

JAN (whispers strangely) Bess?

BESS Yes, Jan ... I'm here.

JAN Are you on this bus too? That's nice.

BESS (confused) Jan wake up—I'm here—what bus?

JAN The 54. I'm sitting at the back. On the next to last seat.
Come here ...

*Jan squeezes her hand. Bess looks at Jan's closed eyes and the sweat
on his brow. He faints. Dodo runs to his aid and starts to ventilate
him by hand. Dr. Richardson prepares the respirator again. He is shaking his head.*

**Scene 136.** EXT. BUS STATION. DAY

*Bess scurries around the bus station, looking at the numbers of the
buses. She is just about to give up when the 54 rolls up. She looks at it
for a while, unsure of herself. She turns to leave. She almost bumps
into Dr. Richardson as he passes with his shopping. He looks at her.*

DR. RICHARDSON Hallo, Bess!

BESS (shyly) Hallo.

DR. RICHARDSON I'd like to talk to you ...

*Bess shrugs her shoulders. Dr. Richardson moves closer to her. At that
instant the driver of the 54 releases his brakes. Bess turns round and
hops aboard.*

BESS This is my bus.

*Dr. Richardson watches her depart.*

**Scene 137.** PANORAMA SCENE

*A tiny dot in the distance, the bus makes its way through the moun-
tain landscape. Day.*

**Scene 138.** INT. BUS. DAY

*There are a few passengers at the front of the bus. The rear seats are
all vacant. A couple of kids get on. Later, a man in filthy overalls gets
onto the bus. He looks at Bess on his way to the back of the bus. Bess
ignores him. Nobody else gets on at the next couple of stops. Bess
makes up her mind. She sits down beside the man. He looks at her in
surprise. She sits there for a while without looking at him. She opens*

*his flies. He is confused. He looks round uncomfortably. She slips her hand into his open fly. She jerks him off with her hand. Nobody else notices. An elderly lady turns round and looks at them briefly, but looks quickly away again. He reaches out for her. She removes his hands firmly. The man closes his eyes. Afterwards she wipes her hands on his scarf with contempt, and gets off at the next stop.*

**Scene 139**. EXT. BUS STOP. DAY
*The bus pulls away. She is alone in the middle of the big field between the mountains. She looks dejected. Suddenly Bess is vomiting. She is down on all fours. Then she wipes her lips and clasps her hands.*
BESS Dear God, I have sinned.
> (The gruff voice) Mary Magdalene sinned too, yet she is among my dearly beloved.
*She notices a rabbit watching her. It twitches its nose, sits there perfectly still, watches her. She twitches her lips at it. It puts its head to one side. Bess smiles. She begins to walk home along the road.*

**Scene 140**. PANORAMA SCENE
*Bess is a tiny dot on the road through the mountains. The clouds scudding across the countryside cast sailing shadows on the mountainsides. Day.*

**Scene 141**. INT. HOSPITAL. JAN'S ROOM. NIGHT
*Bess is sitting still in her chair. She is relating the incident on the bus. Jan is listening, his eyes mostly closed still in the respirator. Bess is trying to cheer him up with her story.*
BESS ... you are so huge you're almost bursting out of your pants ... I undo your fly ... I touch you ... I am touching your ... prick ...
*Bess looks impatiently at Jan for some response. He is motionless, his eyes closed in pain.*
BESS (shaken) ... you are breathing so heavily ... I can feel your heart thumping ...

**Scene 142**. PANORAMA SCENE
*The foreground is the empty bell tower on the roof of the church;*

*behind it the great flocks of sheep by the lake. Day.*
**Scene 143**. INT. CHURCH. DAY
*Dodo and Bess are at a church service. They are singing.*
BESS Have you been in to see Jan tonight?
*Dodo nods. They sing again.*
BESS How is he?
DODO Better.
BESS Better?
DODO Just a bit.
BESS Oh ...
*They sing again. Bess closes her eyes.*

**Scene 144**. INT. HOSPITAL. CORRIDOR. NIGHT
*Hastening down the corridor, Bess meets Dr. Richardson.*
DR. RICHARDSON Your prayers have been worth it ... we've
   been able to take him off the respirator ... isn't that nice?
*Dr. Richardson gives her a smile. He strokes her cheek and gazes into
her eyes. Bess avoids his gaze. She goes into Jan's room.*
*Dr. Richardson watches her go.*

**Scene 145**. INT. HOSPITAL. JAN'S ROOM. NIGHT
*Jan sees Bess. He smiles wearily. Bess is beside him at once. She caresses his face with her fingers. He kisses them. He is earnest.*
JAN I was so far gone ... I had to let go completely and the dreams
   came tumbling down towards me ... maybe it's all that medi-
   cine. Dreams I have never had before. You are part of them
   Bess. But they are dark dreams too ... do you think we turn
   into different people when we are close to the edge? Do you
   think that we turn bad when we are going to die?
BESS You're not going to die ... I know you're not. I promise.

**Scene 146**. INT. HOSPITAL. NURSING STATION. DAY
*Dodo and Dr. Richardson are having supper.*
DR. RICHARDSON Some scar tissue has formed as a result of his
   operation. That's what caused the build-up of fluid.
DODO Could it happen again?

DR. RICHARDSON Yes.
*Dodo nods.*

**Scene 147** EXT. CHURCH. DAY
*Terry and Pits arrive in Jan's car. They pick up Dodo and Bess from
church. Terry and Pits josh in the car. Bess smiles at them. Such mer-
riment is lovely. Dodo is carrying her bible. They get into the car. They
drive up across the mountains.*

**Scene 148.** EXT. AT THE SEA SIDE. DAY
*Dodo and Bess get out of the car. Terry has brought a picnic. The four
of them sit down and eat. Bess is cheerful. She sits on her own with
Dodo. Dodo feels uncomfortable.*
DODO You're cheerful today ...
BESS Yes?
DODO Perhaps you shouldn't get your hopes up too high ...
BESS What have you heard?
DODO Dr. Richardson says Jan may get worse again.
*Bess sits for a while as Dodo packs up the picnic things.*
BESS I'm the one who saved his life. I can save it again.
DODO Are you nuts? What do you mean?
BESS I told Jan stories. Stories about love. It was almost like being
    together, him and me. Love can save Jan. He must not forget
    about love. He told me that.
*Dodo looks at Bess and shakes her head.*
DODO What's got into your head this time? Don't let him gain
    any more power over you. Sickness is a mighty power.
BESS I've saved Jan.
DODO Are you stupid enough to believe that?
BESS You always said I wasn't stupid.
DODO You're stupid if that's what you believe.
BESS (sniffs) Why are you saying I'm stupid now?
DODO You can't stop me telling you when I can see you're on
    your way into your world of make-believe again. I said you
    weren't stupid because I could see how hurt you were when
    people called you that. It made me mad that they called you

91

stupid. But you are stupid. Sometimes you are even too stupid to be responsible for your own life.

BESS (furious) And why am I stupid?

DODO You can't even read!

BESS I can, too!

*Dodo considers, and then she gets out her bible. She opens it. She finds a passage and hands the book to Bess.*

DODO Right. Read this. If you can!

BESS (hesitantly) Where is it from?

DODO Psalm 119.

BESS (slowly) 'Blessed are the undefiled in the way, who walk in the law of the Lord. Blessed are they that keep his testimonies, And that seek him with the whole heart.' OK?

*Bess smiles and looks up.*

BESS You still say I can't read?

DODO (smiles lightly) I tricked you. I didn't open it at psalm 119. I opened it at Job. You just know it all by heart!

*Bess looks down at the book again in fright. She looks up at Dodo, dumbfounded. Then she throws the book to the ground and runs away. Dodo is left standing there, unyielding.*

**Scene 149.** EXT. AT THE SEA SIDE. DAY
*Dodo is following a narrow path that goes down behind the great cliffs. The wind has got up. There is rain in the air.*

DODO (shouts) BESS! BESS!

**Scene 150.** EXT. BESIDE LOW ROCKS. DAY
*Dodo finds Bess right at the water's edge. Bess is standing there, the spume from the waves filling the air around her in the howling gale.*

DODO Bess! Time to go!

*Bess turns to face her.*

BESS (radiating certainty) You can tease me if you like. Jan will get well. I know that now. I made a sacrifice and he will get well.

**Scene 151.** PANORAMA SCENE
*Distant waves breaking against rocky coast. Day.*

**Scene 152.**PANORAMA SCENE

*Waves breaking against cavity-riddled rocks. Spume in the air. Day.*

**Scene 153.** INT. HOSPITAL. JAN'S ROOM. NIGHT

*Dr. Richardson is standing in Jan's room. Dodo fusses around Jan a bit. Jan is dosing. Bess is there.*

DR. RICHARDSON (to Bess) We'll be putting a drain in this afternoon. You wait and see—it'll be much easier to get through to him.

*Bess looks up at him in fright.*

DR. RICHARDSON (smiles) Don't worry, it's a very minor operation.

*Dodo gives Jan an injection. Jan opens his eyes and looks at Bess. He looks more malicious than we've ever seen.*

JAN Are you trying to make me feel guilty?

*Bess stands up in fright.*

BESS No, ... what makes you say that?

*Jan looks at Dr. Richardson and Dodo.*

JAN I do believe she wants me to feel guilty!

*Dodo looks mortified. Dr. Richardson finishes off and goes out. Dodo doesn't know whether to stay or leave.*

JAN (to Bess, sharply) I want a word with you!

*Bess comes up to him.*

JAN You look fucking awful. Those crappy clothes you're wearing aren't fit for a woman. You want to shame me by going round dressed like a widow? And me not even dead yet?

*Bess looks like a whipped dog.*

JAN Or maybe you wish I was dead?

BESS No, no, no ...

JAN Well you haven't done what I asked, that's for sure.

BESS I have!

JAN I asked you to be with a man ...

BESS I've done that.

*Bess's voice cracks.*

JAN You call that being with a man? If you don't come too, the whole thing's a joke. Then it is not love.

**Bess** You can't ask that of me. I love you, not some other man ...

**Jan** If you really love me, prove it!

*Bess leans on the bed for support.*

**Jan** (on his way back into his drug-induced high) ... what you need is a man who's strong ...

*Dodo looks at Bess as if she can't believe her own ears.*


**Scene 154.** INT. HOSPITAL. SLUICE ROOM. NIGHT

*Dodo pulls Bess into a sluice room and locks the door. Dodo is furious. She slaps Bess hard. She pants a bit and then slaps Bess again. Bess takes the blows. She stands there and puts her hand to her cheek.*

**Dodo** Are you out of your mind? What kind of game are you playing? Are you going round fucking other men to feed his sick fantasies?

*Bess speaks feebly.*

**Bess** But he did get better ...

**Dodo** He didn't get better. That's the way it goes. Up and down ... he didn't get better—oh, maybe inside your tiny mind he did.

**Bess** (puffing out her chest) He is my husband and God has said I must honour him.

**Dodo** If that's what it means, there's something I've got all wrong.

**Bess** Well, you don't come from round here, do you?

**Dodo** No, and I'm glad I don't. Hearing the locals talk to each other makes you cringe.

**Bess** But you live here, and you go to the church.

**Dodo** Yes, but that doesn't mean I don't look at things my way. My God doesn't speak Gaelic!

**Bess** (het up) Why don't you move then? Your husband is dead.

**Dodo** I'm quite happy where I am ... it's more likely I'd have moved if he hadn't died. A woman has to choose for herself.

**Bess** Dodo!

*Dodo collects herself.*

**Dodo** It's all inside your stupid little head. What you do won't affect Jan either way, whatever he tells you! Wake up, for God's sake! The man has a massive scar in his brain and he's up to the eyeballs in drugs. He hasn't the slightest idea what he's saying!

**Scene 155.** INT. CHURCH. VESTIBULE. DAY
*Bess is washing the floor.*

BESS ... A woman has to choose for herself ... but I don't under
 stand what he is saying ... it's as if someone else is speaking
 inside him ... as if there is good and evil in him at the same
 time.
 (In the gruff voice) If you love him surely you must take the
 good with the evil ... after all, he's only human.
 (In her own voice) Am I doing right?
 (The gruff voice) If what you do is out of love, it's the right
 thing ... If you are doing it for Jan ...
 (Her own voice) But am I damning myself?
 (The gruff voice) Whom do you want to save? Yourself? Or
 Jan?

*The minister comes by with Bess' mother.*

MINISTER It's been a long time, Bess ... most unlike you. I must warn
 you that the Lord looks with anger upon those who fail him.

*Bess smiles apologetically and scrubs away, while her mother looks at
her angrily.*


**Scene 156.** INT. STEPS AT SYBILLA'S. DAY
*Bess rings Sybilla's doorbell. Sybilla answers the door sleepily, in her
dressing gown. She sees it's Bess and embraces her.*

SYBILLA You poor wee pet ...

BESS You've got to lend me something to wear.

*Sybilla nods as she hugs her.*

*(Suggested music: 'Speed King', Deep Purple.)*


**Scene 157.** INT. OPERATING THEATRE. DAY
*Jan is being prepared for his operation by Dodo.*


**Scene 158.** EXT. CONVERTED PUB. DAY
*Bess approaches a rather seedy converted pub, tottering on her high*

*heels. She has parked her moped by the road.*

**Scene 159**. INT. OPERATING THEATRE. DAY
*Dodo administers the anaesthetic with another nurse. Dodo holds Jan's hand as he falls asleep. Dodo takes his pulse.*

**Scene 160**. EXT. CONVERTED PUB. DAY
*A few people are there, mainly men. Bess sits at the bar, drinking slightly nervously, but she's got some attention. She sees a man. He's quite big, an oil worker probably. She picks up her drink and moves to his table. She sits down and drinks. He is looking at her for a time. She looks at the drink.*
MAN How much, love?
*Bess turns to him smiling.*

**Scene 161**. INT. OPERATING THEATRE. DAY
*Dr. Richardson begins the operation. He makes an incision in the skin around one of the holes drilled in Jan's skull.*

**Scene 162**. EXT. ROAD. DAY
*Bess has given the man a lift on her moped and they drive up towards a light-house and other buildings outside the town. An elder from the church sees them from the side of the road.*

**Scene 163**. INT. OPERATING THEATRE. DAY
*Dr. Richardson pushes a cannula into the hole and attaches a thin plastic tube.*

**Scene 164**. EXT. SCRUBLAND BY LIGHTHOUSE. DAY
*Bess and the man have physical sex on the ground. They have not undressed. Bess is clawing him to her, wanting to feel him.*

**Scene 165**. INT. OPERATING THEATRE. DAY
*The anaesthetist spots a sudden fall in Jan's pulse. He administers an injection. The heart trace on the monitor flattens. The team prepare rapidly for resuscitation.*

**Scene 166.** EXT. SCRUBLAND BY LIGHTHOUSE. DAY

*The man fucks Bess violently. Bess opens her eyes and watches the land-scape and the birdcliffs. She looks dully into the sky. Bess is in a daze.*

**Scene 167.** INT. OPERATING THEATRE. DAY

*Jan's body jolts upwards at the shock from the paddles. Injections are administered. His heart fails to restart.*

**Scene 168.** EXT. SCRUBLAND BY LIGHTHOUSE. DAY

*Bess closes her eyes. She clings to the man. She slips in and out of total surrender. She will not let herself go.*

**Scene 169.** INT. OPERATING THEATRE. DAY

*For the second time Jan's body jolts upwards at the shock from the paddles. The atmosphere is hectic. Still no life. Dodo looks at Jan's face.*

**Scene 170.** EXT. SCRUBLAND BY LIGHTHOUSE. DAY

*Suddenly Bess's body is gripped in the throes of an incredibly violent orgasm. She screams.*

**Scene 171.** INT. OPERATING THEATRE. DAY

*At the final attempt, Jan's heart restarts. Dodo looks at his big body as its condition stabilises.*

**Scene 172.** PANORAMA SCENE

*LS of fellside with birds, the birds shooting into the air at Bess's scream. Day.*

**Scene 173.** PANORAMA SCENE

*LS of the lighthouse and the edge of bird fell. Bess is still screaming. Vast flocks of birds rise towards the sky. Day.*

**Scene 174.** PANORAMA SCENE

*LS of town where the flocks of birds are fluttering in the air.*

**Scene 175.** PANORAMA SCENE *The church viewed from above with the flocks of birds in the foreground. Day.*

**Scene 176.** INT. CHURCH. CHURCH HALL. NIGHT
*The council of elders are sitting in silence. The elders are looking at William, who sits there with his eyes glued to the table.*

**Scene 177.** INT. HOSPITAL. CORRIDORS. NIGHT
*Bess limps up in her high heels, heading for Jan's room. She sees Dr. Richardson and Dodo talking. They look at her and the clothes she's in. She passes wide of them on her way towards Jan's door.*
**DR. RICHARDSON** (after Bess) I think it's time we had a little chat.
*Without turning to face him, Bess waves her hand in doubt as she walks away from them.*
**DR. RICHARDSON** Dodo and I have been talking about you ...
*Bess goes through the door into Jan's room.*

**Scene 178.** INT. HOSPITAL. JAN'S ROOM. NIGHT
*Bess is sitting beside Jan's bed.*
**BESS** ... you were so good to me yesterday ... so good and strong as you used to be.
*She is silent now. His eyes are closed, but he is awake. He is on the respirator. Now he opens his eyes and looks up at the ceiling. The tears are running down his cheeks. Jan writes on his pad, 'Let me die'.*
**BESS** No.
*Bess shakes her head.*
**BESS** I'll never let you die.
*Jan writes, 'I am dangerous ... you mustn't come here any more ...'*
**BESS** I'll never let you down.
*Jan is slipping away. He can hardly write now.*
*'... Ashamed ... evil ... in head ...'*
**BESS** I love you. No matter what is in your head.
*Terry comes in. He sees them and remains silent. Jan looks pleadingly at Terry.*

**Scene 179.** INT. HOSPITAL. CORRIDOR. NIGHT

*Terry embraces Bess. They stand in the corridor in each other's arms for a long time.*


**Scene 180.** INT. BESS'S MOTHER'S HOUSE. KITCHEN. DAY

*Dodo and Bess are doing the dishes. In perfect silence. Bess occasionally looks beseechingly at Dodo. Dodo spurns her mutely.*

**BESS** I did it.

**DODO** (crossly) Did what?

**BESS** Saved Jan when his heart stopped yesterday.

**DODO** What are you talking about?

**BESS** I felt it. It wasn't the electric shocks. It was me.

**DODO** Replying to your nonsense is a waste of breath.

**BESS** Oh, didn't you have to use the paddles on Jan yesterday? When his heart stopped during the operation?

**DODO** Bess, Jan's heart didn't stop yesterday. It was a teeny weenie operation. There were no complications whatsoever. As you know very well.

*Dodo goes on washing up. Bess looks confused. Bess's mother comes in.*

**BESS'S MOTHER** I want a word with Bess. On her own.

*Dodo looks at Bess, and then she goes out. Bess's mother looks grave.*

**BESS'S MOTHER** I'm not going to ask what you've been getting up to because I don't want to hear you lie to me. But while you are living under my roof you are to behave like a decent human being.

*Bess lowers her eyes.*

**BESS** I have never lied to you.

**BESS'S MOTHER** (sharply) Did you understand what I just said?

**BESS** (quietly) Yes, mother.

**BESS'S MOTHER** Your grand-father can no longer hold his hand over you with the elders. I don't know if you realise what they can do to you? You have no idea what it means to be cast out. You'll have nothing. Nothing, Bess! I have seen strong men and women wither away after being cast out. You are not strong, Bess. You are a feeble girl. It would kill you, Bess.

*Bess's mother goes out. Bess is left with the washing up.*

**Scene 181**. INT. BESS'S MOTHER'S HOUSE. HALL. DAY

*Dodo opens the door. Dr. Richardson is standing on the doorstep. She lets him in.*

DR. RICHARDSON  Can I talk to her now?

DODO  (knowing all about it) Just a moment.

*Dodo shows him into the parlour. Dodo brings Bess in. Dodo leaves them, shutting the door behind her.*

DR. RICHARDSON  Hallo, Bess.

BESS  Hallo.

DR. RICHARDSON  Can we sit down?

*Bess nods mutely. They sit down.*

DR. RICHARDSON  (collects his thoughts, then smiles) Bess, I think you've got yourself into something that is out of your control ...

BESS  Have I.

DR. RICHARDSON  Are you just a wee bairn the way Dodo says you are?

*Bess looks down at the carpet without replying.*

DR. RICHARDSON  Damn it Bess, he's forcing you to get screwed by every Tom, Dick and Harry ... It's just not you! You can't let someone dictate to you the way he is doing.

BESS  I choose for myself.

DR. RICHARDSON  Choose what?

BESS  To give Jan his dreams.

DR. RICHARDSON  By being screwed by anything with a dick?

BESS  I don't make love with them, I make love with Jan. And I save him from dying.

DR. RICHARDSON  (laughs) I don't deny that verbal sex may act as a stimulant ... so what you are really saying is that your 'sex life' is rather more sophisticated than I'd have believed. Well excuse me, but he seems more like a dirty old man who wants to play the peeping Tom.

BESS  (lost in thought) Sometimes I don't even have to tell him about it.

(Smiles) Jan and me have a spiritual contact.

*Dr. Richardson shakes his head and smiles.*

**BESS** (in her own thoughts) God gives everyone something to be good at. But he wants us to find out for ourselves what it is. I have always been a stupid. But I'm good at this.

*Bess beams at Dr. Richardson.*

**BESS** God gives everyone a talent!

**DR. RICHARDSON** (shrugs) OK. What's mine, then?

**BESS** I don't know. Have you found it yet?

**DR. RICHARDSON** (crossly) What's Jan's talent?

**BESS** (exalted) He is ...

(thinks) ... a great lover!

*Bess beams up at Dr. Richardson.*

**DR. RICHARDSON** I see. And what's your talent then, Bess? Because surely it can't be being screwed by men you've never seen before?

**BESS** (earnestly) I can believe!

*Dr. Richardson sits there for a while. Then he gets up and paces up and down. She looks up at him.*

**BESS** Are you angry now?

**DR. RICHARDSON** Yes, I am angry ... because you can't see that he is messing you about. He's the one who's sick ... what he is doing to you is sick ... and it's getting sicker and sicker ... he is becoming more and more of a danger to you the more the fluid rises in his head.

*He seizes her and pulls her to her feet.*

**DR. RICHARDSON** Listen to me for God's sake!

*Bess looks at him calmly.*

**BESS** Do you always get so involved in your patients problems, Dr. Richardson?

**DR. RICHARDSON** Listen to me Bess. I care for you ...

*He looks at her helplessly for a moment. Then he says very quietly ...*

**DR. RICHARDSON** I love you, Bess ... you are very special ...

*She looks him up and down. Then she opens the door and calls out.*

**BESS** Dodo!

*Dodo comes in.*

**BESS** Will you show Dr. Richardson out?

*Bess looks at him.*

**BESS**  Don't come here again.

*Dr. Richardson shakes his head.*

**DR. RICHARDSON**  What's going to happen now, Bess? Has he told you any more of the 'thoughts' he's had, any more services for you to perform?

*He looks at Bess, who stays silent.*

**DR. RICHARDSON**  Oh, he has, has he? And what's it to be this time? What are you going to give him to slobber over this time?

*Bess looks at him coldly.*

**BESS**  (strong) Please leave.

*Dodo looks at them both. Dr. Richardson realises he won't get any further. He goes through the door. Dodo follows. Bess suddenly looks scared.*


**Scene 182**. INT. CHURCH. DAY

*Bess is kneeling. She is alone.*

**BESS**  Dear Father in Heaven, please tell me what is going on?

*Bess remains silent for a while. It's as if there is no answer.*

**BESS**  Dear Father ... where are you? Oh, do answer me, please!

*Bess looks around in confusion.*


**Scene 183.** EXT. CHURCH. DAY

*Bess tries to start her moped. It won't start. Finally she has to pedal it away.*


**Scene 184.** PANORAMA SCENE

*LS of the road away from the church, with Bess pedalling along towards the town. Evening.*


**Scene 185.** INT. HARBOUR. CAFETERIA. EVENING

*Bess is in the almost deserted cafeteria. A charlady looks at her over her bucket. Bess is in Sybilla's clothes. She has had a Coca-Cola. She is looking out of the window at the quay. Three scantily-dressed girls are waiting for a motor launch. They clamber down into it and sail out in the direction of the big ships lying at anchor further out. The*

107

*man in the motorboat rings a little bell. The girls are taken aboard.*

**Scene 186.** INT. HOSPITAL. JAN'S ROOM. EVENING
*Dodo and Dr. Richardson are in Jan's room. Dr. Richardson looks at Jan's file.*

**DR. RICHARDSON** (to Jan) How are you?

**JAN** (with a crooked smile) I've felt better.

**DR. RICHARDSON** Yes. Unfortunately the periods in which we can get through to you have lately become very rare. I'll have to send you back to Glasgow for a while, I'm afraid.

**JAN** I don't want any more operations.

**DR. RICHARDSON** No. I thought you might take that line. Of course it's entirely up to you. But I have to say that your condition is unlikely to improve without surgery.

*Dodo looks at Jan, who seems determined.*

**DR. RICHARDSON** Well, if you have made up your mind on that point, it may be time to consider other matters. I mean we should start worrying about other people than just you.

**JAN** Bess?

**DR. RICHARDSON** I'm glad you understand what I'm driving at. Do you want to help her?

**JAN** Yes.

**DR. RICHARDSON** Good. Your condition has been very hard on her. I can't judge why, but she is suffering from delusions regarding your condition. To be blunt, I don't think seeing you is good for her.

**JAN** No, it seems not.

**DR. RICHARDSON** She was hospitalised once before, and I am convinced that the best thing we can do for her right now is to admit her again.

**JAN** Where?

**DR. RICHARDSON** As far away as possible.

**JAN** You think that's necessary?

**DR. RICHARDSON** Listen, if you don't want surgery, the indications are that we will enter a prolonged period in which you will be more and more affected by your condition. The poorlier

you are, the more detrimental your influence on her.

JAN (closes his eyes) What am I to do?

DR. RICHARDSON I have drawn up some papers giving me the authority to detain her under the provisions of the Mental Health Act. But I'll need your consent.

*Dodo looks at Dr. Richardson in fright.*

DODO You are going to 'section' Bess?

DR. RICHARDSON It's the only way I can get her treated.

*Dr. Richardson hands a series of documents to Jan. He puts a pen into Jan's hand. Jan looks up at Dodo for a while, the pen in his hand.*

JAN Tell me, Dr. Richardson: will this mean that I will never see her again?

DR. RICHARDSON To be realistic: yes.

*Jan hesitates. Dodo looks at him but doesn't know what to say.*

DR. RICHARDSON You said you wanted to help Bess.

*Jan looks at Dodo, who doesn't know what to think. Then he signs.*


Scene 187. PANORAMA SCENE

*LS of harbour and fjord. A number of ships at anchor, their lights twinkling in the dusk. A big red trawler dominates the shot. Evening.*


Scene 188. EXT. HARBOUR. EVENING

*Bess is on the quay when the motor launch returns. She talks to the ugly little man at the helm.*

BESS How much is the fare out to the ships?

UGLY MAN I can't take you out there, the other girls will flay me.

BESS They can't do all the ships, they don't have time.

UGLY MAN Maybe not.

BESS What about that red one?

UGLY MAN I don't go out to that one any more. She often puts in here, but the girls won't go aboard.

BESS Then you can take me, and no harm done?

*The man shrugs.*

*(Suggested music: 'Stairway to Heaven', Led Zeppelin. Underlies the following scenes. The music fades in and out. Concludes on Ext. Church. Morning: Dodo runs past the children).*


110

**Scene 189**. EXT. MOTOR LAUNCH. EVENING

*Bess is standing in the launch, looking out at the red trawler as they sail towards it.*


**Scene 190**. EXT. RED TRAWLER. EVENING

*Bess looks up at the red vessel from the launch. The man rings the bell. A youngish sailor in a filthy boiler-suit appears. He looks at Bess in the choppy sea. He stares for a while, then drops a rope ladder. Bess leaves her coat in the launch.*

**BESS** How will I get back?

*Bess looks down at the ugly man.*

**UGLY MAN** I'll keep an eye out for you.


**Scene 191**. INT. RED TRAWLER. NIGHT

*In the bowels of the trawler, the youngish sailor leads Bess to a middle-aged man in his vest. They look at Bess for a while. The older man lights a cigarette.*

**MIDDLE-AGED MAN** What can you do?

**BESS** What do you want?

**MIDDLE-AGED MAN** I want you to do it with the sailor.

**BESS** OK.

**MIDDLE-AGED MAN** While I watch.

**BESS** OK.

*Bess goes up to the sailor.*

**BESS** Hallo, sailor.

*The sailor unbuttons his boiler-suit. He seizes her and pushes her down onto a bunk. They roll over so she is on top. He kisses her neck. Bess smiles.*

**BESS** Are you in a hurry?

*They lie there for a while. The middle-aged man watches from his seat. Then he gets up and comes towards them.*

**MIDDLE-AGED MAN** Having fun?

*Suddenly he is holding a knife. Rapidly he slashes Bess across the shoulder. She screams in pain. The sailor tugs her down to him again.*

**YONGISH SAILOR** Stay still!

*Bess twists round and looks at the middle-aged man, who is standing* over them, holding the knife. Blood runs down her neck. She is in a daze.

BESS No! No!

*The sailor pulls her down again.*

YONGISH SAILOR Stay still I said!

*Bess seems to wake up. She becomes terribly angry. She aims and kicks as hard as she can at the crutch of the man with the knife. He collapses to the floor with a bellow. Out of the corner of her eye she notices a pistol that has fallen out of his pocket. The sailor pulls her upright and punches her in the face. She tumbles to the floor and lies there for a second. She is close to the pistol in the semi-darkness. She leaps and grabs it. She points it feverishly at the sailor as he slowly comes towards her.*

BESS I'll shoot you!

*She backs towards the door.*

YONGISH SAILOR You will? You think so?

*He follows her. She manages to get the door open behind her. She reverses out. As she makes to close the door, his hand comes towards her. She whacks it with the pistol handle. He yells, but she pushes the big bolt home, and stumbles up the steps.*

YONGISH SAILOR (yells from the cabin) Nobody will believe anything a hooker says ... nobody will believe you ...


**Scene 192.** EXT. RED TRAWLER. NIGHT

*Bess waves hectically for the motor launch as she listens for signs of life on board. Infinitely slowly the launch approaches through the rain. She scrambles down the rope ladder in shock. The man looks at her shoulder and at the gun. She doesn't deign to look at him. She gasps for air. She lets the rain wash over her face on the trip through the waves to the quay. Finally she drapes her coat round her shoulders.*


**Scene 193.** INT. CHURCH. DAY

*Service. The sermon. Bess tiptoes in. She has the coat round her, but she looks dreadful. The people among whom she sits down edge away and whisper. The minister walks around, pointing out various men, who stand up and pray in Gaelic. The priest passes Bess. He notices her, but feigns indifference. He puts out his hand to point at an old man next to Bess. She grabs his arm and makes his finger point at her. She gets to her feet Her voice is feeble.*

**BESS** Dear God, thank you for your divine gift of love. Thank you for the love which makes man out of man. Dear God ...

*People get to their feet in protest. The priest cuts her off.*

**MINISTER** No woman speaks here! Bess McNiell, the council of elders has decided this day that henceforth you shall no longer have access to this church. They who know you shall not know you. Be gone, Bess McNiell, from the house of God!

*She stands there as if she has not understood his words. Two of the elders have risen and approached. They lead her out. She whispers on the way.*

**BESS** Dear God, please hear me ...


**Scene 194**. EXT. HOSPITAL. DAY
*Bess runs up the steps outside the hospital.*


**Scene 195.** INT. HOSPITAL. JAN'S ROOM. DAY
*Bess looks around the empty room. She peers into the corridor and leaves the room. There is nobody about.*


**Scene 196.** INT. HOSPITAL. CORRIDORS. DAY
*Bess sees Jan being wheeled into a room far along the corridor. She runs towards it. Dodo comes round a corner with two policemen. They block her path.*

**POLICE OFFICER** Hallo, Bess.

*Bess looks at the policemen, but wants to get past them down to where Jan is.*

**POLICE OFFICER** (smiles gently) You're coming with us, Bess. You are going to Glasgow.

*Bess looks at Dodo. Bess shakes her head.*

**DODO** You're going into hospital again. It's for your own good, Bess.

**BESS** I want to see Jan! I want to see my husband!

**DODO** No, Bess.

**BESS** Mother can't have me admitted … not now I'm married.

**DODO** Your mother didn't sign the papers, Bess. Jan did. He knows how ill you are.

**BESS** You liar!

*The policeman steps up and takes Bess firmly by the arm.*

**POLICE OFFICER** Come along, Bess.

**BESS** (shouts) Jan! JAN!

*They lead her off down the corridor.*

**BESS** (to Dodo) How can you do this, Dodo? You once had a husband too. Your love could have saved him … if only you'd trie …

*Dodo lowers her eyes.*

### Scene 197. INT. POLICE CAR IN COUNTRYSIDE. NIGHT

*Bess is on the rear seat in the moving car. The two policemen are in the front. She looks at the reflecting streetlight on the seat. She lies down, exhausted, and closes her eyes.*

### Scene 198. EXT. HELIPORT. NIGHT

*The policemen are standing beside the car, talking. They look through the window at Bess, who is sound asleep on the back seat. They put a coat over her. She is sleeping like a baby.*

### Scene 199. PANORAMA SCENE

*LS of shipyard and heliport with lights on. The helicopter, engine thudding, appears from over the mountains and lands. Night.*

### Scene 200. EXT. HELIPORT. NIGHT

*The helicopter is at rest. The policemen walk out to it. They talk to the pilot. One policeman returns to the car to fetch Bess. The back seat is empty. He looks round in the dark.*

### Scene 201. INT. DR. RICHARDSON'S FLAT. STAIRS AND LANDING. NIGHT

*Dr. Richardson comes home and goes up the stairs. Rain is lashing the windowpane. He is about to let himself in when he notices Bess, who is curled up in a corner, asleep and soaked to the skin. He wakes her up.*

**Scene 202.** INT. DR. RICHARDSON'S FLAT. NIGHT

*Dr. Richardson makes Bess a cup of tea. She drinks it.*

**BESS** Don't send me away to hospital.

**DR. RICHARDSON** I have to, Bess.

**BESS** Didn't you say that you were different from the old doctor?

**DR. RICHARDSON** I have to do it, Bess.

**BESS** (nods) Then Jan will die.

**DR. RICHARDSON** (smiles) Do you think so?

**BESS** (nods) Yes.

**DR. RICHARDSON** Then let me at least save you.

**BESS** Don't you realise that I have died already? When I made up
my mind to follow Jan, I died. It is too cold here for love. It is
too cold here ... and now I am all alone ...

*Dr. Richardson puts his arm round her. He draws her close. She reacts
to his touch with revulsion. She gets up and moves away from the
table.*

**BESS** Don't touch me!

*Dr. Richardson gets up and comes towards her.*

**DR. RICHARDSON** Bess ...

*Bess gets the pistol out of her pocket. She points it at him.*

**BESS** Touch me again and I'll kill you.

*Bess runs out down the stairs.*


**Scene 203.** EXT. STREETS. MORNING

*Bess is on her way home on her moped. She comes down the street in
her hooker gear. Kids congregate round her. She smiles at them wearily.*

**A BOY** (shouts) Who's a tart!

*The others laugh. They close round Bess. She doesn't like it. She
accelerates. One kid picks up a handful of pebbles and throws them at
her. They hurt. More stones strike her. The kids run along behind her.*

**KIDS** (chant) Who's a tart! Who's a tart!


**Scene 204.** EXT. BESS'S MOTHER'S HOUSE. MORNING

*Bess fumbles for her key. She finds it and pokes it into the keyhole, but
she can't open the door. The door has been bolted.*

**BESS** (scared) Open the door! ... I can't open the door!

*The children are now at the garden gate.*
BESS Mother, mother, open the door, oh please mother ...

## Scene 205. INT. BESS'S MOTHER'S HOUSE. MORNING
*In the living room mother is sitting silently and upright on a chair. Dodo is also sitting there. She looks wretched. She looks pleadingly at Bess's mother, who shakes her head sternly.*

## Scene 206. EXT. BESS'S MOTHER'S HOUSE. MORNING
*Bess is still banging at the door. A clod of soil whistles past her ear from the street.*
BESS Oh mother please open the door, please, please ... I'll be really good, really, really good ...
*Bess deflates. She'll have to run the gauntlet of the children again. She picks up her moped and runs out. She forces her way through the congregated kids.*

## Scene 207. EXT. STREETS. MORNING
*Bess manages to get onto her moped and pedals it away as quick as she can. The kids follow her. Chase her.*

## Scene 208. EXT. COUNTRYSIDE. MORNING
*Bess is still being pursued by stones and mud. She is pedalling laboriously now. On the verge of falling off. She is helpless.*

## Scene 209. EXT. CHURCH. MORNING
*Bess has to run, pulling the moped up to the church. The children are screaming on her heels. Suddenly she stops, right outside the church. She stands there for a second. The children hesitate. Then she faints. She collapses onto the little square. The children step back a bit.*

## Scene 210. INT. MINISTER'S HOUSE. MORNING
*The minister sees everything from his window. He stands there for a moment, and then goes outside.*

**Scene 211**. EXT. CHURCH. MORNING

*The priest chases the children away.*

MINISTER Go away! Stop all this racket outside the house of God!

*The children retire slowly down the road. The minister glances at Bess, prone on the ground. He feels the children's eyes are on him from down the road. He quickly goes inside again.*


**Scene 212.** INT. BESS'S MOTHER'S HOUSE. MORNING

*Dodo gets up slowly and silently. Bess's mother stands in the doorway in her path. Dodo puts her coat and scarf on.*

BESS´S MOTHER You're not going!

*Dodo looks at her briefly. Then she shoves her aside and runs out.*


**Scene 213.** EXT. COUNTRYSIDE. MORNING

*Dodo runs towards the church.*


**Scene 214.** EXT. CHURCH. MORNING

*Dodo runs past the children to the church. The minister is looking out of his window. Dodo reaches Bess, who is still prone. Dodo helps her to sit up. She squeezes her hand.*

DODO Little Bessie ...

*Bess comes round a bit.*

DODO (in despair) Oh, little Bess ... I wasn't to tell you, but Jan is dying now. No more can be done ...

*Bess looks up at her calmly.*

DODO They said you mustn't be told, but now I've told you anyway ...

*Bess smiles feebly.*

BESS Good you did ... thank you Dodo, I know you love me.

*Dodo cries. Bess holds her.*

BESS I must go now.

*Dodo clings to her.*

DODO What can I do to help?

BESS (smiles) Nothing ...

*Bess thinks.*

**BESS**  Well, I'd like you to go to Jan ... and pray. Will you do that for me?

**DODO**  Of course I will.

**BESS**  Pray for him to be cured and to rise from his bed and walk.

*Dodo nods. Bess gets up laboriously and brushes off her clothes. She picks up the moped. She tries the pedals, but they're stuck. She wheels the moped along. It makes a scraping sound. The children make way as she walks through the crowd. Dodo watches her.*

**Scene 215.** PANORAMA SCENE
*LS of harbour and fjord. The red trawler is still there. Day.*

**Scene 216.** EXT. HARBOUR. DAY
*Bess is sitting down, watching the sea-gulls. The ugly man in the motor launch arrives. He moors just below where she is sitting. He looks up at her.*

**BESS**  I'd like to go out to the red boat.

*The ugly man looks at her in disbelief.*

**UGLY MAN**  I'm not going anywhere. Come again tonight.

*Slowly she climbs down into the boat and sits down. The ugly man scowls and they set off.*

**UGLY MAN**  Didn't you get enough last time?

**Scene 217.** EXT. MOTOR LAUNCH. DAY
*Bess is standing in the prow as the launch works its way towards the red trawler.*

**BESS**  Dear Father, why aren't you with me?
(Gruff voice) I am with you, Bessie. What do you want from me?
(Astonished, in her own voice) Where were you?
(Gruff voice) Don't you think I have anyone else who needs to talk to me?
(Smiles, in her own voice) Of course, I hadn't thought of that.
(Gruff voice) There's this daft little thing called Bess who keeps on wanting me to listen to her, so my work's been piling up a bit.
(Smiles, in her own voice) Not daft, funny ...

122

(Gruff voice) ... funny little thing ...

(In her own voice, laughing at first, but then dubious) But you're with me now?

(Gruff voice) Of course I am, Bess.

(In her own voice, tears in her eyes) Oh, good. I am glad.

*The ugly man looks at Bess, who's talking to herself.*

## Scene 218. EXT. RED TRAWLER. DECK. DAY

*Bess climbs aboard. The middle-aged man and the sailor look at her suspiciously.*

## Scene 219. INT. RED TRAWLER. CABIN. DAY

*Bess is sitting on the bunk in the cabin. She undresses slowly. She looks at a reflection of the sun in the water outside that is projected onto the ceiling. She does not sense the rough action taking place around her. We only see a close up of her. She is being screwed with a knife at her throat. She is being thrown around. She is still just looking at the reflection.*

## Scene 220. INT. HOSPITAL. INTENSIVE CARE. NIGHT

*Dodo comes into where Jan is lying. The only sound is the respirator. Dodo looks at Jan for a while. Jan is silent. The door opens and Dr. Richardson comes in. Dodo looks up.*

**DODO** Oh, sorry, do you need me?

**DR. RICHARDSON** No, no, you can stay here.

*They stand there for a while, without speaking. Then Dodo pulls herself together.*

**DODO** Bess asked me to pray ...

**DR. RICHARDSON** For what?

**DODO** For Jan's life ... for a miracle.

**DR. RICHARDSON** (smiles) Yes, that really would be a miracle.

*Dr. Richardson goes out. Dodo kneels. She looks at Jan. He is motionless.*

**DODO** Dear God let Jan get better ... let him rise from his bed and walk ...

*Jan doesn't move.*

**Scene 221.** EXT. RED TRAWLER. NIGHT

*Bess is being lowered down the side of the ship to the motor launch. She is tied to a stretcher. Her eyes are closed. The launch is crowded with police and ambulance-men.*

UGLY MAN She was taking so long. I dinna like it.

*The ugly man is talking to a policeman. Now the launch heads for the quay and the waiting ambulance.*

**Scene 222.** INT. AMBULANCE. NIGHT

*Bess is lying on the stretcher. The ambulance is on the road along the coast. Her eyes are closed.*

**Scene 223.** INT. HOSPITAL. NURSING STATION. NIGHT

*Dodo receives a telephone call. She jumps in fright.*

**Scene 224.** PANORAMA SCENE

*LS of town sea front and road. The ambulance hurtles past the buildings with its lights flashing and siren wailing. Night.*

**Scene 225.** INT. HOSPITAL. CORRIDORS. NIGHT

*Bess is wheeled rapidly along corridors to the surgical ward.*

**Scene 226.** INT. HOSPITAL. OUTSIDE OPERATING THEATRES. NIGHT

*Dodo runs up. She takes Bess by the hand.*

DODO My poor darling ...

*Bess is wheeled into an examination room.*

**Scene 227.** INT. HOSPITAL. EXAMINATION ROOM. NIGHT

*A doctor cuts Bess's bloody clothes off. Dr. Richardson comes in. Dodo looks in horror at her battered body.*

DODO Who did this?

BESS Me and nobody else.

*Bess's voice is weak. Dodo looks up impotently at Dr. Richardson as he examines her. He shakes his head hopelessly.*

DODO Don't worry, we'll make you better again.

*Bess smiles, her eyes closed.*

BESS Shhh ... Dodo, you know that's not true ...

*She opens her eyes now, gravely, and looks at Dodo while the doctors prepare her for surgery.*

BESS Just tell me how Jan is doing?

DODO Oh Bess, you know he's dying ...

BESS Isn't he any better?

DODO No, Bess, no.

BESS Oh?

*Bess closes her eyes.*

BESS I thought he might be better now ...

*She opens her eyes again.*

BESS Where is he? I'd like to see him.

*Dodo looks interrogatively at Dr. Richardson, who shakes his head.*

DODO Not yet, Bess, you need an operation now.

BESS (her face twists in pain) Dodo I've got to see Jan ... I've got
    to ...

DODO (to Dr. Richardson) Just a moment ...

*Dodo runs to the door to the corridor. People have crowded round. Dodo shoves them aside.*

DODO Go away for Christs sake!

*Dodo runs across the corridor and opens the door into intensive care. She runs back to where Bess is lying and helps her turn her head a little so she can see Jan, who is lying motionless in the respirator. The crowd in the corridor look at Jan and Bess, too. Bess looks at Jan for a long, long moment. Her eyes flood with tears. She clings to Dodo's arm.*

BESS Oh Dodo ... maybe I was all wrong after all!

*Bess sees her mother standing behind some people in the corridor. Bess smiles.*

BESS Mother!

*Bess' mother comes up to her.*

BESS Mother I'am sorry that I could not be good.

BESS'S MOTHER It's alright Bessie.

*She stands close to her daughter for a while.*

BESS'S MOTHER Your grandfather couldn't come.

BESS (smiles) Of course not. Please tell him that I love him. I am glad that you came Mother.

*Suddenly Bess is out of breath. Dodo leans over her.*

BESS Dodo, hold me.

*Dodo holds her tight.*

BESS (whispers) I'm frightened.

DODO I know, my pet.

*Bess shakes her head.*

BESS Oh, Jan ... I'M FRIGHTENED ... IT'S ALL WRONG ...

*Her body slackens. Dodo shakes her head.*

DODO No, no ... Bessie ... my wee pet ...

*Dodo starts crying hysterically. The doctor puts his arms round her. In intensive care, Jan is lying in the respirator, motionless.*

### Scene 228. PANORAMA SCENE

*LS sunrise in the mountains. The valleys are covered in clouds, and only the peaks rear up. Morning.*

### Scene 229. PANORAMA SCENE

*The sheep are running about in the hill fog. The sunrise has lent the whole scene the most fantastic colours. Morning.*

### Scene 230. PANORAMA SCENE

*LS of church; all that is visible is the bell tower—the rest is shrouded in the low cloud. Morning.*

### Scene 231. INT. CHURCH. CHURCH HALL. MORNING

*The council of elders is meeting again. William is in his place, disconsolate. There is utter silence.*

CHAIRMAN I think that everything there is to say about Bess McNiell has been said. We have decided to inter her, but there'll be no funeral service. The fact that a number of us knew the deceased girl well will in no way influence the form of her interment. Bess McNiell will be buried in just the same fashion as anyone else of her kind.

CHAIRMAN (looks at a letter) The corpse will be released by the

127

authorities sometime this week.

*The minister gets up and goes out.*


**Scene 232.** INT. CHURCH. VESTIBULE. MORNING

*The minister closes the door quietly behind him. He goes over to Jan, who is sitting in a wheelchair. Dodo is holding the wheelchair. Jan looks up at the priest without a word.*

MINISTER (quietly) I've obtained the elders permission to inter Bess, but ...

*The minister hesitates for a second.*

MINISTER (with a glance at Dodo) ... but I cannot deviate from the principles that apply to funerals here.

JAN You knew her well. You were like family.

MINISTER It makes no difference.

JAN So when you bury Bess, you will damn her too? And say that she is going to hell?

MINISTER I have to follow the rules laid down by the council of elders. I must say about Bess what must be said.

*Jan sits in thought for a moment. Dodo looks down. Jan nods. The minister goes out. Dodo wraps the rug round Jan's legs. She wheels him outside.*


**Scene 233.** INT. CORONER'S COURT. DAY

*The inquest in the little coroner's court. Dr. Richardson is testifying. The coroner is examining some papers.*

CORONER You have described the deceased as 'an immature, unstable person. A person who, due to the trauma of her husband's illness, gave way in obsessive fashion to an exaggerated, perverse form of sexuality'. The court would like a more detailed explanation, Dr. Richardson.

DR. RICHARDSON (sits in silence for a moment) Did I write that?

CORONER (looks at the papers) That's what it says.

DR. RICHARDSON (clears his throat) I should like to amend my statement.

CORONER New evidence has arisen, Dr. Richardson?

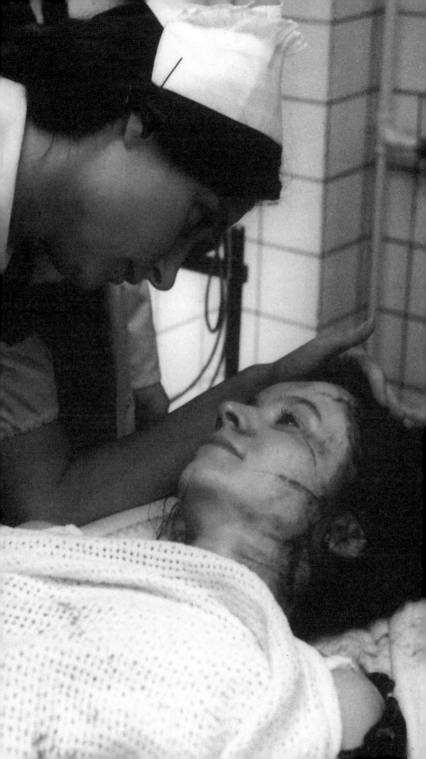

DR. RICHARDSON No, but ... May I have a glass of water?

*Dr. Richardson does not feel well.*

CORONER Give Dr. Richardson a glass of water.

*An officer of the court pours a glass of water and hands it to Dr. Richardson. Dr. Richardson drinks.*

CORONER Listen, man, you had the deceased in your care, and the court would like to hear the medical facts.

DR. RICHARDSON Facts? Allow me to say that according to everything I have read or been taught, I have written an exhaustive conclusion. Nobody can deny it. And yet ...

CORONER Yes?

DR. RICHARDSON I beg your indulgence. I have been bed-ridden the last couple of days and may still be coloured by my fever. This case has affected me profoundly, and if you asked me know, instead of 'neurotic' or 'psychotic', my diagnosis might quite simply be ... 'good'!

CORONER Good?

DR. RICHARDSON Yes.

CORONER You wish the records of this court to state that from the medical point of view the deceased was suffering from being 'good'?

*Dr. Richardson sits in silence.*

CORONER Perhaps this was the psychological defect that led to her death? Is that what we shall write, Dr. Richardson?

*The judge looks at Dr. Richardson ironically. Dr. Richardson shuts his eyes.*

DR. RICHARDSON (feebly) No, no ... of course not.

CORONER Well then, shouldn't we stick to your original statement, Dr. Richardson?

DR. RICHARDSON (nods) Ah, quite, that would probably be best.

*Dr. Richardson glances down at the members of the public. Jan is in his wheelchair beside Dodo.*


Scene 234. EXT. CEMETERY. DAY

*Jan limps across the cemetery on two crutches. The weather is beauti-*

*ful. He stops and looks at the family grave.*

**Scene 235.** PANORAMA SCENE

*In the distance we see Jan and Terry standing on a little patch of sand on the otherwise stony beach. Jan's car is parked on a road down to the water. Jan is digging. The wind is blowing. Evening.*

**Scene 236.** INT. SMALL CHAPEL AT CEMETERY. NIGHT

*Bess's coffin is resting on a couple of trestles in the chapel. It is night. Terry fumbles as he tries to pick the lock. He succeeds. He and Jan enter. Terry opens the coffin and looks at Bess. She doesn't appear on camera. Jan averts his eyes.*

**Scene 237.** EXT. CEMETERY/CAR PARK NEXT TO CEMETERY. DAY

*There is a gale blowing. The minister is performing the rites. Some seagulls screech in the wind. We see that the only people at the interment are the twelve old men. The minister's clothes flap in the wind. The twelve men stand there oppressively and silently. A little way away in the cars beyond the fence, Dodo and Bess's mother are sitting with the other women. Dodo is weeping with Sybilla, who is in the same car. Dr. Richardson is there, too. He is in the cemetery himself, but at a distance from the grave. He is weeping. Dodo keeps looking around. She turns to Sybilla.*

**DODO** (whispers) Where's Jan?

*Sybilla shakes her head. The coffin is being lowered. Dodo jumps out of the car and runs to the graveside. The others don't acknowledge her presence.*

**MINISTER** (quietly) Bess McNiell, you are a sinner and for your sins you are consigned to hell.

**DODO** (shakes her head) No one of you has the right to consign Bess to hell.

*The elders look at Dodo. None of them moves. They continue to lower the coffin. Dodo goes right to the edge of the grave and peers down. She is the only one to spot a trickle of sand from a joint as the coffin tilts slightly. She doesn't say a word. Now she looks out to sea.*

### Scene 238. PANORAMA SCENE

*Far below us, infinitely small, a supply ship is fighting through the towering waves. The sea toys with the little vessel and casts it hither and thither. Day.*

### Scene 239. INT. CABIN ON SUPPLY SHIP. DAY

*Jan has to hold on tight so as not to be thrown around the cabin. He is staring into space. The water is up to the little port-hole. Bess is strapped to the bunk. Bess's face is pale and serene. Her body is thrown from side to side in the straps. Jan hides his face in his hands. Terry comes in. He looks gravely at Jan.*

TERRY We'll be there soon.

*Jan nods quietly. He looks up at Terry.*

JAN I tore her from her home and her family ... do you think she can forgive me for that?

TERRY It's time, Jan.

### Scene 240. EXT. SUPPLY SHIP. DECK. DAY

*Jan and Terry struggle with the big packing case. Jan is impeded by his crutches. They manage to fasten it to the hook dangling from the crane on the rig, The supply ship is in danger so close to the steel legs. The packing case rises. It takes a couple of hefty knocks before it is free in the air. Jan and Terry climb into the lift basket. Terry shouts to Jan as they ascend through the gale.*

TERRY When shall we do it?

JAN Not in this weather ... I don't want her to come to any harm.

### Scene 241. INT. RIG. JAN'S CABIN. MORNING

*Jan is asleep in his cabin. Morning has come and there is utter silence. Jan wakes up and looks out to sea. It's foggy. It's half past five. Jan gets up.*

### Scene 242. EXT. RIG. LITTLE DECK. MORNING

*Jan, Terry and Pits pull the crate across the little deck. They position it by the railings. They are about to pull Bess out when Jan pushes them aside and lifts her out by himself. It is hard for him. He puts her gently* onto the lid of the crate, which is resting on the railings. Pits looks around anxiously, but there is nobody about. Terry looks worried.

TERRY  Get a bloody move on!

JAN  I have to say a few words.

*He clasps his hands. He speaks slowly.*

JAN  Dear God, I've never known you or talked to you before … I don't know what people usually say …

*His eyes brim with tears.*

JAN  … Take good care of her …

*Jan is sobbing. He leans over her and kisses her. He doesn't want to let go. Terry pulls him away from her. He nods to Pits, who lifts the wooden lid. Bess slides off and drops towards the waves. She vanishes in the fog. The three men are left there in silence.*


**Scene 243.** INT. RIG. JAN'S CABIN. DAY

*Jan is lying on his bunk, staring at the ceiling. The fog can be seen through the window. He closes his eyes. He lies there for a while. Then there is a quiet knock on the door. Terry comes in.*

TERRY  I know you're knackered … but you've got to see this.

*Jan shrugs. He pulls on his trousers.*


**Scene 244.** INT. RIG. RADAR ROOM. DAY

*Terry leads Jan into the radar room. A couple of men are already gazing intensely at the screen. Terry looks at Jan, who looks at the screen.*

TERRY  Well, what do you see?

JAN  (shakes his head) Nothing. Not a ship. We're alone on this damned island of steel in the middle of the sea. So what?

*Terry nods.*

TERRY  I just wanted to be sure you agreed.

JAN  (crossly) What's all this about?

TERRY  Come with me. It's bloody fantastic.

*Terry leads Jan out of the room.*


**Scene 245.** EXT. RIG. BIG DECK. DAY

*Terry leads Jan out onto the big deck, where Pits is waiting. The air is vibrating with the sound of great bronze church bells. Many of the crew have already taken up position. They are standing quietly, listening. Many are gazing into the fog. Jan looks up, too. The sound of the bells is huge.*

**Scene 246.** PANORAMA SCENE
*Deep beneath us lies the oil rig. It is almost indiscernible in the fog. The bells resound in the air about us. Day.*

**Scene 247**. PANORAMA SCENE
*We are in an assemblage of clouds in which everything is sailing in the wind. The ringing of the bells is louder now. Day.*

**Scene 248.** PANORAMA SCENE
*Hovering high above the billowing cloudscape the two great church bells hang in a super CU foreground, gleaming as the sun strikes their burnished bronze, thundering away to an unseen hand. As if for a funeral.*
*(Suggested music: 'Life on Mars'. Bowie. Underlying.)*


CLOSING TITLES


(NOTE: In this version of the script, medical lines said during the operations and prayers and ritual/biblical lines, in Gaelic/English in the church, have been omitted.)

# LOCATION LIST

**STUDIO**

DET DANSKE FILMSTUDIE,
Blomstervænget 52, DK-2800 Lyngby, Denmark

| | |
|---|---|
| Int. Rig. Jan's Cabin | scenes: 62, 69, 75, 241, 243 |
| Int. Rig. Shower | scenes: 61, 66 |
| Int. Rig. Radio Room | scenes: 68a, 71a |
| Int. Mother's House, | |
| Dodo's room, | |
| Jan's room | scenes: 43, 44, 45, 58, 70, 81, 82, |
| | 99, 102, 104, 110, 111, |
| | 180, |
| | 181a, 205, 212 |
| Int. Hotel Room | scenes: 27, 29 33, 46 |
| Int. Dr.Richardson's Flat | scenes: 127, 128, 129, 202 |
| Int. Hotel. Toilet | scenes: 20 |
| Int. Church | scenes: 2, 14, 15, 28,  31, 32, 56, |
| | 57, |
| | 79, 94, 107, 108, 125, |
| | 143, 155, 76, 182, 193, |
| | 231 |

## LOCATIONS DENMARK

HELA, Sydhavnen, København
Int. Trawler                          scene: 191

KØBENHAVNS KOMMUNE HOSPITAL
Øster Farimagsgade 5, 1399 Kbh.K
   Hospital. Glasgow          scenes: 85, 86, 88, 89, 90. 91,
                                         115, 36

MARINE CLUB
Enghavevej 64, 1674 Kbh.V
   Wempi Bar                   scene: 92

ULRIKKENBORG ALLÉ
2800 Lyngby
   Dr. Richardson's Landing    scenes: 126, 201, 202a

LYNGE KRO
Højrisvej 22-24, 3540 Lynge
Small Cinema                          scene: 36
Court Room                            scene: 233
Hotel Assembly Room                   scenes: 17, 18, 21, 22, 22a (19),
                                         23, 73, 102

AMTSSYGEHUSET I GENTOFTE
N. Andersensvej 65, 2900 Hellerup
Local Hospital                        scenes: 96, 97, 98, 100, 101, 102,
                                         103, 112, 113, 114, 116,
                                         117,118, 119 120. 121, 122,
                                         123, 132, 133, 134, 135,
                                         141, 144, 145, 146, 153,
                                         154, 157, 159, 161, 163a,
                                         165, 167, 169, 171, 177,
                                         178, 179, 186, 195, 196,
                                         220, 223, 225, 226, 227

RIGSHOSPITALET
Blegdamsvej 9, 2100 Kbh.Ø
Hospital/Operating Theatre          scene: 163b


NORTH SEA
Ext.Oil rig.                        scene: 248
Oil rig. Staircasenew scene: Jan running up
    the staircase to phone
Supply Ship Esbjerg Havn            scene: 239


**LOCATIONS SCOTLAND**


BARMAC
NIGG,
TAIN,
ROSS-SHIRE IV19 1QY
Shipyard                   scenes: 48, 49, 51
Heliport/Int.Helicopter    scenes: 4, 12, 52, 53, 54, 83, 84


TREASURE DRILLER / WILRIG
Departure from Cromarty Firth Port Authority
Shore Road, Invergordon, Ross-shire IV 18 OHD
Oil Rig                    scenes: 67,  68a,  71a,  242,  244,
                                   245, 246


MONTROSE FIRE & EMERGENCY TRAINING CENTER
Forties Road, Montrose D10 9ET
Oil Rig                    scenes: 50, 60, 60a, 64, 80, 102-
103


MALLAIG HIGHLAND
    Ext. Hotel,
    The Marine Hotel       scene: 47
    Converted Pub,
    The Marine Hotel       scenes:  158, 160, 192a
                                    (new scene)

| | |
|---|---|
| Bus Stop | scene: 136 |
| Harbour / Ext. Trawler | scenes: 185, 188, 189, 190, 192, 216, 217, 218, 198, 200, 203, 221a |
| Ext. Mother's House | scenes: 82a, 109,181, 204, 206 |
| Ext. Sibylla's Home | scene: 156 |
| Ext. Minister's House | scene: 210, 214a |
| Playground | scene: 105 |
| Street | scenes 207 |
| Ext. Hospital, | |
| Mallaig High School | scenes: 95a, 194 |
| Ext. Hotel | |
| Glasnarcardoch Hotel | scene: 24 |
| Seaside, Morar | scene: 235a |

## POLNISH CHURCH
Roman Catholic Diocese of Argyll & the Isles, Lochailort

| | |
|---|---|
| Ext. Church | scenes: 3, 16, 28a (new scene), 30, 63, 65, 68, 71, 76, 78, 95, 147, 183, 192b (new scene), 209, 210, 211, 214, 214a, 232 |

## NEIST POINT LIGHT HOUSE
Glendale, Isle of Skye

| | |
|---|---|
| Ext. Lighthouse | scenes: 1, 148a, 149, 150, 162, 164, 166, 168, 170 |
| Cemetery | scenes: 37, 39, 106, 234, 237a |
| Parking Lot | scenes: 38, 40, 41, 148, 237 |

## ROAD BETWEEN UIG AND STAFFIN
Isle of Skye

| | |
|---|---|
| Int/Ext. Bus | scenes: 138, 139 |
| Countryside | scenes: 124, 208, 213 |

# BIOGRAPHICAL NOTES

**EMILY WATSON plays BESS**

LONDON BORN ACTRESS EMILY WATSON studied English Literature at Bristol University before attending The Drama Studio in London for a year's post-graduate course. She has since worked at the Royal Shakespeare Company, with directors including Sir Peter Hall, as well as appearing at the Royal National Theatre and in regional repetory. Director Christopher Morahan cast her in her first television role in A SUMMER DAY'S DREAM, playing the role of the granddaughter of Sir John Gielgud.

Making her film debut as Bess, Emily plays the naive and deeply religious girl who finds a love which plunges her into eroticism and eventual sacrifice that she never dreamt could exist. Her taking the part was an act of faith in Lars von Trier as a director. 'The scenes are so emotional, so on the edge, that I have to become swept away by the character's passion, and put my trust in Lars that he is guiding us all in the right direction.' says Emily, 'It's too hard to stand outside Bess and judge her, as an actress. There has to be commitment to Bess' passion. It's not easy, but it is rewarding.'

'Emily is a real discovery,' commented von Trier. 'The instant she began screen testing, in a particularly difficult scene that would not normally be chosen for the purpose, I knew she was Bess.'

## STELLAN SKARSGÅRD plays JAN

AS A FAMILY MAN BASED IN STOCKHOLM, actor Stellan Skarsgård is able to relate to those men who work away from home on the rigs. 'As actors who travel where the jobs are, working long hours, in a mainly male environment, we can experience the isolation from family and friends felt by those oil rig workers. Although, of course, we live in much more comfort than they do, there is still a sense of isolation, and many hours spent on the phone to the family at home.' He describes his character Jan as a man 'who's been around, who can't believe that he has found a woman with Bess' purity and he feels maybe he doesn't deserve her love.' Skarsgård praised von Trier's working methods. 'The use of handheld camera gives Lars the freedom to let a take continue until it reaches a natural end, which is much more satisfying for an actor than the short sharp takes usually used to cover a scene.'

Skarsgård spent sixteen years as part of the company of the Royal Dramatic Theatre in Stockholm, working with Scandinavia's finest directors in a variety of classic plays. At 16, he became a household name in Sweden after appearing as the lead in the TV series Bombi Bitt, but his international breakthrough came in Hans Alfredson's THE SIMPLE-MINDED MURDERER, for which he won the Best Actor Silver Bear in 1982 at the Berlin Film Festival. He has won awards for his performances in Carl Gustaf Nykvist's WOMEN ON THE ROOF, HIPP HIPP HURRAH! and GOOD EVENING, MR WALLENBERG, both directed by Kjell Grede. Other Scandinavian film roles include two appearances playing Carl Hamilton, the Swedish superagent, for director Pelle Berglund, and the lead in Bjørn Runge's HARRY AND SONJA (1996). Skarsgård has worked with international directors Philip Kaufman in THE UNBEARABLE LIGHTNESS OF BEING and John McTiernan in THE HUNT FOR RED OCTOBER.

### KATRIN CARTLIDGE plays DODO

AS BESS' OVERPROTECTIVE and recently widowed sister-in-law, Katrin Cartlidge welcomed the chance to play a more restrained role than is usually required of her. 'Dodo thinks she is in control, and is accustomed to being Bess' protector. When Jan comes along she is frightened of how the outside world will affect Bess, who is ill-equipped to deal with it, and, as a widow, she is jealous of their relationship.'

Katrin Cartlidge won international recognition, including the award for European Actress of the Year and European Press Prize for Best Actress, when she appeared in Mike Leigh's award-winning film NAKED. Since then she has gone on to work with exciting new directors, including Milcho Manchevski, whose film BEFORE THE RAIN was winner of the 1994 Golden Lion at Venice Film Festival, and Constantin Gianaris director of THREE STEPS TO HEAVEN, (invited to screen at Director's Fortnight at Cannes Film Festival in 1995).

Cartlidge joined the Royal Court Youth Theatre while still at school and spent time on the London and Edinburgh fringe theatre. She has worked at the Royal Court, and extensively at the Royal National Theatre as well as appearing in an assortment of roles on British television.

### JEAN-MARC BARR plays TERRY

FRENCH-AMERICAN ACTOR JEAN-MARC BARR was happy to accept when von Trier offered him the part of Terry, a friend and Jan's workmate on the oil-rig. Barr hails von Trier as a revolutionary direc-tor, who uses a novel style of story telling and is unafraid to tackle new technology and to present a challenge to his audiences.

Born in Germany, Barr trained as an actor at the Guildhall School in London and enjoys a truly international career. Here he rejoins director von Trier, following his lead role in EUROPA, a film he considers to be the finest he has ever done and a role he accepted in preference to Hollywood films he was offered after starring in the international success, Luc Besson's THE BIG BLUE (1988).

Having made his film debut in Bruce Beresford's epic KING DAVID (1985), Barr prefers roles with more European sensibilities, and his appearances include John Boorman's HOPE AND GLORY (1987), Luis Puenza's adaptation of the Camus classic tale THE PLAGUE (1992).

### UDO KIER
### plays THE MAN ON THE TRAWLER

UDO KIER, WHO PLAYS THE BRUTAL MAN on the trawler, a sadist, whom Bess uses to engineer the final sacrifice in her efforts to save Jan's life, is one of von Trier's favourite actors, having already appeared for the director in EPIDEMIC and EUROPA, as well as THE KINGDOM.

Kier's career started in 1969 in the German splatter movie THE TORTURE CHAMBER OF THE WITCH HUNTER. Among the directors who have made use of his talents since then, Fassbinder figures most prominently, but Paul Morrisey and Gus van Sant are also on the list. Kier appeared in MY OWN PRIVATE IDAHO (1991) and EVEN COWGIRLS GET THE BLUES (1993). He will next be seen in BARB WIRE, starring Baywatch babe Pamela Anderson and has a major role in Steve Barron's live action PINOCCHIO.

**ADRIAN RAWLINS**
plays **DOCTOR RICHARDSON**

As THE KINDLY LOCAL DOCTOR, Dr. Richardson is anxious to help Bess and in the end feels commital to a mental hospital is necessary for her own physical and mental safety.

Adrian Rawlins is a familiar face on British stage and television. After gaining a degree in Creative Arts at Crewe College, he became involved in performance arts, touring with his own company for two years. His extensive theatre credits include spells at the  Royal Exchange Theatre Manchester and a variety of roles at the Royal National Theatre. In addition to television appearances, his film credits include REVOLUTION, for director Hugh Hudson and MOUNTAINS OF THE MOON, directed by Bob Rafelson.

**JONATHAN HACKETT**
plays **THE MINISTER**

As THE SHEPHERD OF HIS FLOCK, the Minister often seems harsh and unforgiving in the penalties he sees it as his duty to hand out to those whom the Church decides have broken its strict rules.

Although born in Scotland, Jonathan Hackett moved to London as a teenager to pursue a career as a cabaret artist and moved on to work on the stage before concentrating on television and film work. His film credits stretch from Richard Attenborough's award-winning A BRIDGE TOO FAR in 1977 to FIRST KNIGHT in 1995, directed by Jerry Zukor. As a writer he has dramatised, for the stage, the novels THE COUNT OF MONTE CRISTO and LITTLE WOMEN, both performed at the Royal Exchange Theatre, Manchester.

**SANDRA VOE plays BESS' MOTHER**

BESS' MOTHER HAS LOST HER SON on the oil rigs and tries to keep her family together, but the power of the church is too much for her and when she is eventually compelled to reject Bess she is hurt and bewildered by her daughter's behaviour.

Sandra Voe was born on the Shetland Isles and trained as an actress in Edinburgh. A familiar face on British stage and screen, she has appeared on stage all over Britain for a variety of directors in both classic and modern plays, as well as guest appearances in many UK television series. Best remembered by cinema-goers for her role in LOCAL HERO (1983), she most recently appeared on film in IMMORTAL BELOVED, which starred Gary Oldman as Beethoven.

# CREDITS

EMILY WATSON
STELLAN SKARSGÅRD
KATRIN CARTLIDGE
JEAN-MARC BARR
ADRIAN RAWLINS
JONATHAN HACKETT
SANDRA VOE
and
UDO KIER

| | |
|---|---|
| Pits | MIKKEL GAUP |
| Pim | ROEF RAGAS |
| Grandfather | PHIL McCALL |
| Chairman | ROBERT ROBERTSON |
| An Elder | DESMOND REILLY |
| Sybilla | SARAH GUDGEON |
| Coroner | FINLAY WELSH |
| Glasgow Doctor | DAVID GALLACHER |
| Man on Bus | RAY JEFFRIES |
| Man at Ligthhouse | OWEN KAVANAGH |
| Man on Boat | BOB DOCHERTY |
| Young Sailor | DAVID BATESON |
| Radio Operator | CALLUM CUTHBERTSON |
| Police Offcer 1 | GAVIN MITCHELL |
| Police Officer 2 | BRIAN SMITH |
| Praying Man 1 | IAIN AGNEW |
| Praying Man 2 | CHARLES KEARNEY |
| Praying Man 3 | STEVEN LEACH |
| Nurse | DORTE RØMER |
| Boy 1 | ANTHONY O'DONNELL |
| Boy 2 | JOHN WARK |
| Precentor | RONNIE McKELLAIG |

| | |
|---|---|
| Written and Directed by | **LARS VON TRIER** |
| Producers | **VIBEKE WINDELØV**<br>**PETER AALBÆK JENSEN** |
| Executive Producer | **LARS JÖNSSON** |
| Director of Photography | **ROBBY MÜLLER** |
| Operator | **JEAN-PAUL MEURISSE** |
| Casting | **JOYCE NETTLES** |
| Art Director | **KARL JULIUSSON** |
| Costume Designer | **MANON RASMUSSEN** |
| Sound Designer<br>& Recording Mixer | **PER STREIT** |
| Film Editor | **ANDERS REFN** |
| Executive Music Producer | **RAY WILLIAMS** |
| Music Arranged<br>& Orchestrated by | **JOACHIM HOLBEK** |
| Co-Writers | **PETER ASMUSSEN**<br>**et al.** |
| Co-Producers | **AXEL HELGELAND**<br>**PETER VAN VOGELPOEL**<br>**ROB LANGESTRAAT**<br>**MARIANNE SLOT** |
| 1st Assistant Director | **MORTEN ARNFRED** |

152

| | |
|---|---|
| Unit Production Manager | Lene Nielsen |
| Assistant to the Producers | Charlotte Pedersen |
| Production Manager | Leif Mohlin |
| Location Manager | Morten Kleener |
| Production & Post Production Assistant | Tine Grew Pfeiffer |
| Production Assistants | Casper Holm |
| | Nanna Mailand-Hansen |
| Production Assistant, Paris | Nynne Oldenburg |
| Gaffers | Christopher Porter |
| | Leif Barney Fick |
| Electrician | Søren Johannes Meyer |
| Still Photographer | Rolf Konow |
| Focus Puller | Pim Tjujerman |
| Camera Assistants | Per Fredrik Skiöld |
| | Thomas Holm |
| Property Master | Peter Grant |
| Property | Simone Grau Larsen |
| Property Assistants | Rasmus With |
| | Jonas Alexander Arnby |
| Make-up | Jennifer Jorfald |
| | Sanne Gravfort |
| Special Make-up & Surgical Effects | Morten Jacobsen |
| Make-up Assistant | Dorota Boronska |
| Costume Assistant | Anne-Marie Gudnitz |
| Props Seamstress | Mini Mandal |
| Continuity | Linda Daae |
| Dialogue Coach | Elspeth Macnaughton |
| Boom Operator | Ad Stoop |
| Video Assists | Morten Ziersen |
| | Steve Holtson |
| | Frederik Kihl |
| Photographer - Rigshospitalet | Per Heegaard |
| Runners | John Goodwin |
| | Rasmus Heisterberg |

| | |
|---:|:---|
| Bus Driver | Frank Weinberger |
| Trainees | Birgitte Skov |
| | Niels Reierman |
| Props Trainee | Eva Gøttrup |
| Catering | Charlotte Giannetta |
| | Lange-Møller Catering ApS |
| Additional Casting | Ruth Tarko |
| Casting, Denmark | Rie Hedegaard |
| Assistant to Joyce Nettles | Louise Cross |
| Script Translation | Jonathan Sydenham |
| Script Consultants | Kirsten Bonnén Rask |
| | Tómas Gislason |
| Medical Consultant | Grethe Wejlgaard |
| Folkdance Consultant | Else Hartzberg |
| Church Consultant | Christina MacKay |
| Scottish Music Consultant | Tom Harboe |
| Financial Controller | Charlotte Vinther |
| Production Accounts | Ann Køj Slemming |
| | Ghita Nørrekjær |
| | Ann Vognsen |
| Studio | Det Danske Filmstudie |
| Construction Manager | Leo Jørgart |
| Carpenters | Torben Skallebæk |
| | Poul Erik Andersen |
| | Mogens Craner |
| | Thomas Westi |
| Head Painter | René Pejl |
| Painters | Jørgen Krogh |
| | Søren Simonsen |

## POST PRODUCTION

| | |
|---:|:---|
| Post Production Supervisor | Tove Jystrup |
| Assistant Editor | Anders Johannes Bukh |
| Trailer Editors | Yann Dedet |
| | Lars Wodschow |
| | Niklas Hansen |

| | |
|---|---|
| Graphic Designer | Morten Constantineanu Bak |
| Title Sequence/Photographer | Henrik Jongdahl, DFF |
| Supervising Sound Editor | Kristian Eidnes Andersen |
| Dialogue Editor | Hans Møller |
| FX Editor | Peter Schultz |
| Foley Artist | Julien Naudin |
| Post Syncing 'Ugly Man' | Peter Bensted |
| Post Syncing 'Boy in Film' | Simon Towler Jorfald |
| Sound Studio | MAINSTREAM ApS |

## CHAPTER AND END SEQUENCES

| | |
|---|---|
| Visual Digital Effect | MANIPUTASION |
| Artist | Per Kirkeby |
| Visual Editors | Søren Buus |
| | Steen Lyders Hansen |
| | Niels Valentin Dal |

## SCOTLAND

| | |
|---|---|
| Location Manager | Janet Riddoch |
| Location Scouting | Anthony Dod Mantle |
| | Peter Øvig Knudsen |
| Production Consultant | Christine Maclean |
| Casting, extras | Anne Campbell |
| Costumes | Binkie Darling |
| Additional Property | John Knight |
| Special FX | Lars Andersen |
| Runners | Stephen Burt |
| | Glenn Weinold |
| | Ricki Rasmussen |
| Stunt Coordinator | Terry Forrestal |
| Building Construction | Alistair MacGregor |
| Rig Workers, Montrose | Douglas Brand |
| | William Ryan |
| | Tony English |

**SECOND UNIT**

| | |
|---|---|
| Director | Kristoffer Nyholm |
| Photographer | Eric Kress, DFF |
| Focus Puller | Mads Thomsen |
| Sound Recording | Klas Baggström |

**SFX-CREW**

| | |
|---|---|
| Photographer | Jan Weincke, DFF |
| Focus Puller | Birger Bohm |
| Gaffer | Otto Stenov |
| Public Relations | Hanne Palmquist |
| | Christel Hammer |
| Public Relations Assistant | Nynne Selin |
| Assistant to Mr. Jönsson | Anna Anthony |
| International Public Relations | Corbett & Keene |
| International Sales | World Sales Christa Saredi, Zürich |
| Completion Bond supplied by | Film Finances Ltd., David Wilder |
| Insurance Services provided by | Sedgwick A/S, Jens Georg Hansen |
| Laboratory-Production | Johan Ankerstjerne A/S |
| Negative Cut | Marianne Jerris |
| Laboratory - Post Production | Éclair Laboratoires |
| Colorgrading on Film | Olivier Fontenay |
| Colorgrading on Video | Patrick Dreyfus |
| Video Transfer 35 mm | Ex Camera |
| Digital Video Consultant | Damien Maurel |

**PRODUCED BY**

ZENTROPA ENTERTAINMENTS ApS
IN COLLABORATION WITH
TRUST FILM SVENSKA AB
LIBERATOR PRODUCTIONS S.a.r.l.
ARGUS FILM PRODUKTIE

156

NORTHERN LIGHTS A/S
IN CO-PRODUCTION WITH
LA SEPT CINÉMA
SWEDISH TELEVISION DRAMA
MEDIA INVESTMENT CLUB
(Media Programme of the European Union)
NORDIC FILM- & TELEVISION FUND,
Bengt Forslund and Dag Alveberg
VPRO TELEVISION
SUPPORTED BY
DANISH FILM INSTITUTE, Jørgen Ljungdalh
SWEDISH FILM INSTITUTE, Per Lysander
NORWEGIAN FILM INSTITUTE,
Oddvar Bull Tuhus and Gunnar Svensrud
DUTCH FILM FUND
DUTCH COBO FUND
FINNISH FILM FOUNDATION
Marketing supported by SCALE/STRATEGICS
(Media progamme of the European Union)
Fund of the Council of Europe
Developed with the support of
EUROPEAN SCRIPT FUND
an initiative of the Media programme of the European Union
IN ASSOCIATION WITH
CANAL+ (France)
DR TV
ICELANDIC FILM CORPORATION
LUCKY RED
OCTOBER FILMS
PHILIPPE BOBER
TV 1000
VILLEALFA FILMPRODUCTIONS OY
YLEIS RADIO TV-1, FINLAND
ZDF / ARTE

## MUSIC

Music produced by Pollyanna Music Ltd.

Music Producer
Mark Warrick
Assistant to Ray Williams
Peter Raeburn

### ALL THE WAY FROM MEMPHIS
Performed by: Mott The Hoople
Composed by: Ian Hunter
Courtesy of: Columbia Records
by arrangement with Sony Music
Licensing.
Published by: 1973 Island Music Ltd.

### BLOWIN' IN THE WIND
Performed by: Tom Harboe,
Jan Harboe & Ulrik Corlin
Written by: Bob Dylan
Published by: Special Rider Music /
Sony Music Entertainment Inc. / ATV
Music Publishing

### PIPE MAJOR DONALD MACLEAN
Performed by: Peter Roderick MacLeod
Written by: Peter Roderick MacLeod
Courtesy of: Peter Roderick MacLeod -
MCPS

### IN A BROKEN DREAM
Written & Performed by:
Python Lee Jackson
Featuring: Rod Stewart
Courtesy of: Minder Records
Published by: Minder Music Ltd.

### CROSS EYED MARY
Performed by: Jethro Tull
Written by: Ian Anderson
Courtesy of: Chrysalis Records Ltd
by arrangement with EMI Special Mar-
kets UK
Published by: Salamander & Son Ltd. /
Chrysalis Music Ltd.

### VIRGINIA PLAIN
Performed by: Roxy Music
Courtesy of: Virgin Records Ltd.
Published by: EG Music represented
by BMG Music Publishing, France

### WHITER SHADE OF PALE
Performed by: Procul Harum
Written by: Keith Reid &
Gary Brooker
Courtesy of: Cube Records Ltd.
Published by: Onward Music Ltd.

### HOT LOVE
Performed by: T Rex
Written by: Marc Bolan
Courtesy of: Straight Ahead Producti-
ons Ltd.
Published by: Onward Music Ltd.

### SUZANNE
Performed by: Leonard Cohen
Courtesy of: Columbia Records/Sony
Music Entertainment (Canada)Inc.
Published by: TRO Essex Music Ltd.
### LOVE LIES BLEEDING
Performed by: Elton John
Composed by: Elton John & Bernie
Taupin
Courtesy of: Polygram Music Ltd.
Published by: Dick James Music Ltd.

### GOODBYE YELLOW BRICK ROAD
Performed by: Elton John
Composed by: Elton John & Bernie
Taupin
Courtesy of: Polygram Music Ltd.
Published by: Dick James Music Ltd.

### WHISKY IN THE JAR
Performed by: Thin Lizzy
Composed by: Phil Lynott, Eric Bell &
Brian Downey
Courtesy of: Polygram Music Ltd.
Published by: Pippin the Friendly Ran-
ger Music Ltd. /
Polygram Publishing Ltd.CHILD IN

### TIME
Performed by: Deep Purple
Composed by: Jon Lord, Ritchie
Blackmore, Ian Gillan, Roger Glover &
Ian Paice
Courtesy of: EMI Records Ltd.by
arrangement
with EMI Special Markets UK
Published by: B Feldman & Co. trading
as Hec Music Ltd.

First published in Denmark in 1996
by Forlaget Per Kofod ApS
Nikolaj Plads 32
DK-1067 Copenhagen, Denmark

First published in Great Britain in 1996
by Faber and Faber Limited
3 Queen Square London WCIN 3 AU

Printed in Denmark by Nørhaven A/S, Viborg

© Lars Von Trier and Forlaget Per Kofod ApS, Copenhagen
Denmark, 1996
Translated from the Danish by Jonathan Sydenham
Preface by Stig Björkman translated from the Swedish by
Jonathan Sydenham
This book is published in cooperation with ZENTROPA
Entertainments ApS, Denmark
Design and page make-up by graphic designer Kirsten Sonne, Copenhagen
Cover photograph and stills by Rolf Konow
'Panoramic Scenes' on the flaps by Per Kirkeby

Lars Von Trier is hereby identified as author of this
work in accordance with Section 77 of the Copyright,
Designs and Patents Act 1988

A CIP record for this book
is available from the British Library

ISBN 0-571-19115-0